EIGHT GREAT DREIDEL STORIES

CURRICULUM COLLECTION
RATNER MEDIA CENTER
BUREAU OF JEWISH EDUCATION
2030 South Taylor Road
Cleveland Heights, Ohio 44118

```
CMC      Gal, Martin
244.1    Eight great dreidel
GAL      stories

8061
```

EIGHT GREAT DREIDEL STORIES

MARTIN GAL

ALEF DESIGN GROUP

Copyright © 1994 Martin Gal

                Library of Congress Cataloging-in-Publication Data
    Gal, Martin, 1927–
    Eight great dreidel stories / Martin Gal.
      p. cm.
    ISBN # 1-831283-10-0
    I. Title.
    PS3557.A37E38   1994
    813l.54—dc20   94-23180
                                                        CIP

Published by Alef Design Group
All rights reserved. No part of this publication may be reproduced or transmitted in any form or by any means graphic, electronic or mechanical, including photocopying, recording or by any information storage and retrieval system, without permission in writing from the publisher.

Alef Design Group
4423 Fruitland Avenue
Los Angeles, California 90058
(213) 582-1200

To my only wife, Jean.

*Willing to laugh at my humor,
and care for the moments of sadness,* **too***.*

What else could a writer as for?

TABLE OF CONTENTS

Dreidel Goes to Las Vegas… Unbelievable! 9

The Dreidel Dancer 35

Dreidel Stops Here/Amtrak Doesn't 47

Mark of a Dreidel 63

The Dreidel Maker and the Rich Man 81

Sour Marriage, Sweet Dreidel 89

Song From a Dreidel 113

A Dreidel for Vice President? 139

DREIDEL GOES TO VEGAS...
UNBELIEVABLE!

So, you want another Hanukkah Story? This one goes back a few years. Every detail I can't remember. The ESSENCE? This you'll get. But if I'm wrong here and there a fact or two, forgive me.

First, I never should have trusted Shelly Chance. It sounded too easy. I never trusted him anyway, the way he dressed. Why I trusted him this time…? You could tell I must have been meshuggenah.

Two. If I had to trust him, I should have gone with him, instead of sending that shlump Manny.

Three. I was almost rich. Almost! So I guess I shouldn't complain.

As I said, I didn't trust Shelly. He was a sharp dresser with a white tie always; black hair flat, nothing out of place. The kind of hair that will never get bald, like mine. Now, could you trust such a guy?

DREIDEL GOES TO LAS VEGAS...UNBELIEVABLE!

He always seemed to do well. Never as well as he said he was going to do. But well. He found himself a dreidel, you see, which worked for him better then anyone else. This dreidel he kept in a blue velvet bag with a gold drawstring, a bag from a bottle of Seagrams Royal Crown.

With this dreidel, Shelly would start up a game in the back of Schwartz's Texaco and win. I'd spin and lose. Phil would spin and lose. But Shelly? How did he do it? He won pot after pot.

Let me explain. A regular group we were, with money to burn. Once or twice a week we'd meet in the back of the Texaco. What's more logical than the back of a gas station? You can park fifteen cars outside and no cop suspects. Cars at a gas station? They're waiting to be fixed, right? And the noises from arguments? The curses from winners and losers? Who could hear all that yelling over the sound of an air compressor? A Texaco station, the perfectly safe place to win big. But we didn't win. Shelly won.

Why a dreidel you ask? Because if you are on a hot streak, you can win quicker with a dreidel. Not like poker where you *putz* around waiting for Jake Friedman to slowly peel his cards to see if he's filled an inside straight. Impossible. In Five-Card Draw for instance, Jake will start with one ace, and hope a miracle will deal him three more. You don't believe me, but there are guys that play poker that way. They believe they can fill cockamamie hands. Actually.

And the way some people bet! You'd think they're deciding to invade Moscow! It takes Miltie Kay absolutely an hour to see a four-bit raise. And…but, why bother you with details. Just believe me, to win BIG, a dreidel on the move is tops.

Now this business of Shelly Chance winning all our money? …it had to stop. Or we needed to get a piece of the action. Why should Shelly win so much from friends? Are we made of gold? Of course not.

DREIDEL GOES TO LAS VEGAS...UNBELIEVABLE!

So it was natural we formed a 'syndicate' to send Shelly to Cincinnati, hoping he could win big on strange ground. A syndicate? It's a name we got from the boys who bankrolled Cassius Clay, the boxer, who has since become an Arab. They made a killing by getting in on the ground floor. We raised eight hundred dollars seed money to send him to Cincinnati. With Shelly, we sent Manny Hertzberg to watch over.

Why Manny, you ask? Manny is six foot eight and weighs like a truck. To help you understand, Manny is retired from never working a day in his life. His poor aunt Tillie died in Pittsburgh and left him three brick apartment buildings which the city bought from him to make a Golden Triangle downtown. Manny retired full time. We kid him, but everyone wishes he had an aunt to leave him a Golden Triangle. Money didn't change him. He wore the same messy herringbone sport coat, green and black. You wouldn't buy it for a quarter from the Salvation Army. But Manny always had a dollar in his pocket, if you understand me. Manny, his name in Hebrew is Emanuel, which means "God is with us." So who better to send to Cincinnati to look after our interests?

Manny and Shelly left with our eight hundred on Friday morning. By Sunday night they came back with three thousand, AFTER they took off for expenses! I told you a hot dreidel is quick money! Everyone was amazed. We ordered corned beef brought to the back of the Texaco to discuss our future. The first thing we discussed was for everyone to keep their mouth shut. If Shelly were dealing with a loaded dreidel, God forbid, which I doubt, we wouldn't want anyone to know we were connected with it. One the other hand, if it wasn't fixed and he would win big, we still wouldn't want anyone to know we were connected with it. This is CASH MONEY you understand we're dealing with.

Let me interrupt here, because maybe you're not familiar with a dreidel. It is a four-sided Jewish top. On each side is a Hebrew letter: *Shin,*

DREIDEL GOES TO LAS VEGAS...UNBELIEVABLE!

Gimmel, Hay and *Nun*. Players ante up for each pot. Say the pot is five dollars each. Each person spins the dreidel in turn. When the dreidel stops, the letter tells the spinner what to do. If *Shin*, he must ante up another five dollars. If *Hay* comes up, he takes half the pot. If *Gimmel* comes up, he takes all the pot and everyone antes up again another five dollars. If *Nun* comes up, nothing. That turn is a bust.

What was happening was... Shelly kept coming up *Gimmels*. No one could explain. Was it really fixed, you ask me? How could you fix a dreidel? Everyone in turn spins the same one. You can't put it up your sleeve. How could you fix it? Dreideling is about as fair as Life, which is not exactly a perfect recommendation. But it's the best I can do.

A fixed dreidel! The possibility isn't nice. Who would do such a thing to a Jewish symbol! A fixed dreidel would be *treif,* not kosher. A sacrilege. It is from our holiday Hanukkah. To fix a dreidel would be like the Fleischmann Yeast Company making Matzos. Never! But to get on with it. In two days our eight hundred dollars became three thousand. That's nearly four hundred percent on our investment. Miltie Kay tells me it's really five thousand percent, figured annually. But only he figures that way.

What next? I'll tell you what next. Like it or not. Las Vegas! The "like it" came from Shelly. It was his dreidel and that's where he wanted to go. The "or not" came from Phil Klein, Jake Friedman and me. Las Vegas? Not one of us had been there, but we heard about it. Vegas sharks would eat Shelly alive. Vegas is not Cincinnati. It's big time. The biggest time. On the other hand, if Las Vegas can take Cleveland money, they can probably give it back, too.

The syndicate decided. Vegas. Or better, Shelly decided he was going and we decided to make money instead of arguing. How much did we raise? Even now I'm surprised on short notice. We started with three thousand from the Cincinnati trip. The Blickstein twins talked their Yenta into cashing her Cleveland Trust stock. They told her they were

DREIDEL GOES TO LAS VEGAS...UNBELIEVABLE!

buying a kosher chicken farm. Phil Klein sold his collection of baseball cards for three hundred. I raised from various sources, who shall remain nameless because they still don't know where their money went, nine hundred and twelve dollars cash. Plus a few more guys who don't want to be known.

All in all, from the syndicate we sent Shelly to Las Vegas with seven thousand two hundred dollars. This was so if he hit a cold streak he could still function. And if by luck he should stumble onto a big spender, Shelly could handle any pot. Again we sent Manny Hertzberg along. To shlep for Shelly. To protect him. To knock some sense into him if he started getting careless. Hah, little did we know what kind of protection Manny would be.

All the way to Hopkins Airport, piled into Phil Klein's Lincoln, everybody was giving Shelly advice.

"Check to make sure you got the dreidel. Let's see it for luck."

"Don't bet too much on the first round."

"My advice is if, *kinahora*, you hit twenty thousand quit and bring it home."

"Twenty thousand? Are you crazy. If we get twelve thousand he should quit. It's my Yenta's money."

"What are you talking twelve thousand! We're not sending him to Ashtabula. He's going to Vegas, where the big money is. At least he should win thirty thousand."

"Manny," I said to Hertzberg, "watch over Shelly. Watch nobody steals from us. Vegas is full of *goniffs*."

Through it all sits Shelly, calm as a bullet. You know something is going on inside his head, but nothing shows. This is his big chance, but you'd think we were driving to the corner for a selzter or a beer. To make a long story less, off they go high in the air with all our money.

DREIDEL GOES TO LAS VEGAS...UNBELIEVABLE!

Now I suppose you want to know what happened? What I'm telling you is pieced together from what they told us later in the back of the Texaco, plus maybe a bit here and there filled in from my imagination. After all, we are still hearing some details years later. Manny Hertzberg every once in a while remembers new things.

Vegas. You wouldn't think it would be a surprise. After all you've heard about it. You see travel posters. You think you know what it's going to be like. No. It was half as much. I mean twice at least. Bigger, more money, more guys in expensive suits, more ladies with less, knockout blonds, redheads... everything more than Shelly or Manny could dream of. They rented a room at a place called the Stardust, on the sixth floor because the seventh was more expensive. Lucky, you know.

On his first day Shelly wore yellow pants, a red shirt, the famous white tie and a green striped sportcoat. Vegas should know he was here. The two of them went to give the town a look. And what a look! Neon signs as big as the downtown May Company. Going day and night. Flickering, flashing, winking, arrows up, arrows down, lights going in six directions at once. As if the guy who makes Holiday Inn signs drank a bottle of peppermint schnapps and built Las Vegas before he sobered up. And that's just for starters.

In one place, a circus is going on right in the middle of the slot machines. People are playing blackjack and a gorilla sits down beside them. As Manny said, "If I had a banana, the gorilla could have peeled it for me." That close! Not Cleveland, Ohio by any means.

But in the gambling, you won't believe what surprised them. You know how it is with us in the back of the Texaco. when we play cards, or dreidel, or shoot craps, it's a friendly group. While the cards are dealt, Jake will tell a joke. A laugh here and there never hurts. In Vegas it hurts. Shelly sat at a blackjack table and put down a dollar. In an ice-box voice, the dealer tells him it's a two-dollar minimum. So naturally

DREIDEL GOES TO LAS VEGAS...UNBELIEVABLE!

Shelly throws in another dollar. He says, "This will be like losing twice." Everyone at the table gives him such a look. "From what planet are you, hick?" they are thinking.

The playing goes around. Shelly asks for a hit and busts at twenty-three. In the next round, while the dealer's dealing, Shelly says, "This reminds me of a joke about a Rabbi and a shady lady...." Before he can say another word, the man next door growls.

"Look Buster, if you're a comedian, get booked in the lounge. When you play here, it's with your mouth shut."

You could have knocked Shelly over with a pickle. He gave Manny a look over his shoulder. "What's going on here?" Shelly dumps the next hand with a lady, a six and a seven. Who wants to play cards if it's brain surgery? They go to another table.

Same thing. Shelly tries a little conversation. A *zaftig* redhead tries to take his head off with her alligator purse. She yells at him in language we don't even use in the back of the Texaco. Out of such a beautiful face comes four, five and six letter words you can't translate into Hebrew because it would violate seven of the Ten Commandments. Including some things that are physically impossible.

"What's with this place?" thinks Manny to himself. It's worse than playing in Little Italy back in Cleveland, where nobody likes to lose even temporarily. Here in Vegas, with over seven thousand dollars in their pockets, it's like a foreign country.

Manny went to sit in the bar, hoping to strike up a conversation. "Hey, where you from? Oh, Peoria. Want to play a little dreidel? My friend is getting up a game."

You wouldn't believe the looks he got. Then a large fella in a plain blue suit tried to throw Manny out. But Manny was bigger. He warned Manny, though. "Don't talk like that around here." He could take a hint, so he stopped talking like that.

DREIDEL GOES TO LAS VEGAS...UNBELIEVABLE!

So what to do? They got into a cab.

"Take us to a Jewish neighborhood," said Shelly.

"Is that supposed to be a joke?" asked the driver.

"You heard my friend," said Manny, "Don't you give us a hard time, too."

The driver turned around. He was maybe fifty. "Mister, with all due respect, I'm from Portland, Oregon. I've been in Vegas one month. I wouldn't know a Jewish neighborhood if I got arrested there. I'm a Methodist and my wife's Catholic. Give me a street name and I'll try to find it."

"Drive around downtown," said Shelly. They knew they'd find something. On the way, what amazing buildings they saw. Pink buildings with doors in the shape of hearts. WEDDINGS. 24 HOURS. NO WAITING. Pink and white. 24 hours? Who wants to get married at four in the morning? That's the time to go to bed. The brain at that time isn't thinking straight.

Finally, they arrived. Ten o'clock at night, in front of Pincus' Wild West Delicatessen. You could smell corned beef as the cab turned the corner.

"You smell that?" Manny hits the cab driver on the shoulder, "That's what a Jewish neighborhood smells like."

"You mean garlic?"

"Corned beef!" growls Manny, "If you're ever lost in the desert and you smell that, you know your life is saved."

"We'll walk from here," said Shelly. He handed the driver a five because he felt sorry for a Methodist who never tasted corned beef.

Except for the huge neon lights and the lightbulbs in the shape of silver dollars, this could have been a Jewish neighborhood anywhere. Up the street were the same stores—a One Hour Martinizer cleaners, a Sam's Bakery for fresh bagels and rye, a Cohen's Kosher Meat Market.

DREIDEL GOES TO LAS VEGAS...UNBELIEVABLE!

Some eating paces, The Golden Gelt Sandwich, Irving's Hotsie Pastrami, and Mandelstein's Shalimar Cafe... like a Jewish neighborhood anywhere!

The boys walked around. Shelly bought a tongue and corned beef. He hinted around. Manny ordered mushroom-barley soup at another place. He ate slowly. "Who plays dreidel?"

"A kid's game," says a *putz* with a pencil mustache and two diamond rings.

"So, if you know any rich kids," says Manny, "tell him it costs a hundred bucks to sit in." He left a note with their room number at the Stardust.

In no time word got out there was a new game in town. A Cleveland team, consisting of a smart-aleck and an overweight schmuck who couldn't count. All in all, they made it appear they were going to be easy marks.

Who could resist? Before you know it... a phone call here... a note in the box there... nine guys are in their room at the Stardust by noon the next day. If I told you the money came easy, you wouldn't believe it. But it came easy. Manny started to worry. In twenty-four hours they were fourteen thousand dollars ahead. "Shelly, let's take what we've won and go. I feel funny about this."

"I'm on a hot streak. You wanna take off? Take off. But I came here to make a pile and I'm doing it." Shelly wouldn't budge. On almost every turn Shelly is rolling a *Gimmel* and taking the pot, which is getting bigger because the losers don't know how to become winners except by pushing up the ante. So every *Gimmel* is getting better for Shelly. By noon the first day it costs a hundred to get in. By eight that night it's five hundred. By eleven it takes a thousand to sit down. Who can explain it? It gets to the point where Manny thinks maybe the Dreidel

DREIDEL GOES TO LAS VEGAS...UNBELIEVABLE!

is controlled by a dybbuk, a strange spirit. How else could the winning go on and on?

As the Dreidel is passed around, one guy spins. *Hay.* Put in another thousand. Next to him Mr. Cigar Stump spins. *Hay.* Ante another thousand. The next guy is at least lucky. He spins a *Nun*, which means it costs him nothing to keep losing. On and on around. "Spin, you four-sided *putz*" cries out a lonely voice. But it comes up cold.

Then it's Shelly's turn again. *Gimmel*! The whole pot! They can't believe it.

Ante up all around.

In the door come hotshots. Out the door they leave broke. More take their place. Manny can't believe this. Where is all this money coming from? It's not even Jewish money. In come Ferrinis, O'Briens, Kaluskis… guys who never heard of a dreidel in their lives. But it's eating them all with equal relish.

Only the man in the cream Panama suit stays. He plays some and watches more.

Round the dreidel goes. It's Shelly's turn again. The pot is now at least twelve thousand dollars. Remember the Blickstein twins said come home if we ever win that much. That much! Here it is in a single pot!

"Ah ha," Panama Suit thinks to himself. "I have finally figured out how it works. These two schmucks from Cleveland have a system. Which is that their dreidel is fixed. It has hidden inside an electrical circuit which this Shelly fella switches on…"

He grabs the dreidel out of Shelly's hand. Everybody jumps. Those with guns move their hands inside their suits. Very cooly, Mr. Panama Suit says, "I think Mr. Shelly Chance Wiseguy, that you are bringing to our honest city a crooked dreidel." No! You can hear the quiet. Shelly is smart enough to know you never argue with a heavy loser. They go crazy at the slightest twitch.

DREIDEL GOES TO LAS VEGAS...UNBELIEVABLE!

Mr. Panama Suit holds the dreidel close to a light bulb. Sees nothing. He takes out a jeweler's glass and screws it into his right eye. Like a Yiddish Count. Still he sees nothing. "Uh hunh" he mutters. Everyone breathes together, once. There is no other sound except the "uh hunh-ing" of Mr. Panama Suit.

"Is this the end of my life?" thinks Manny. Maybe there is a mechanism which Shelly switches. If Mr. Panama Suit proves their dreidel is fixed, ten people in this room will gladly toss Shelly and him out the sixth floor window of the Stardust Hotel, and it won't take a vote to do it.

Into the bathroom Mr. Panama Suit takes the dreidel. He runs hot water on it. Why? Back into the room. Still nothing. So has he found something or not! The losers want to know! Mr. Panama Suit holds the dreidel close to his nose. What is he smelling?

"Can I finish my roll?" says Shelly with a casual sneer.

"Not so fast, Cleveland," says Panama Suit, "I'm still deciding." He's deciding? What he isn't counting on is that the dreidel is also deciding.

Panama Suit sit down at the table and spins. The dreidel falls. *Gimmel.* "Ah hah" you say. Wait. He spins again. *Hay.* Again. *Sin.* Again he spins. *Nun.* All four sides. The dreidel goes through its whole act. Each side comes up the same number of times, Exactly. If you have any common sense and aren't already losing, you know this is impossible.

But what of Panama Suit and eighteen suspecting eyes? What will they think of a dreidel which suddenly goes through its paces like a darling child reciting the ABC's over and over?

"I declare," says Panama Suit, "this dreidel is good. Only this *putz* from Cleveland has been lucky. But luck don't last."

What if the dreidel heard Mr. Panama Suit and knew exactly how to put everyone at ease? The next turn for Shelly, what comes up? *Shin.* Shelly kicks in a thousand to the pot. And the next turn for him, another *Shin.* Another thousand lost. And his next turn? *Nun,* for

DREIDEL GOES TO LAS VEGAS...UNBELIEVABLE!

nothing. Meanwhile, three or four *Gimmels* come up for other players, including twice for Mr. Panama Suit. Each time they win, Shelly must ante to a new pot. It appears to all the world that Shelly's luck has run out. The big shots relax. They now KNOW this dreidel is not fixed. A few win back some peanuts here and there. Enough to pull the blanket back over their heads. Then Shelly starts again to knock off *Gimmels*. But their memory is stuck back in history. The first thing a loser loses is his Sekhel, his common sense. He will grab at any cockamamie omen which hints that luck has finally turned his way.

You want me to tell you that behind all this lucky dreideling is some dark and distant spirit? A dybbuk? How can I? Imagine this. A Jew in some distant life played and played and lost his furniture, his home, his wife's silver candlesticks... a loser who finally lost even his life. He believed giving his life would bring him some peace. But it didn't. The LOSING gnawed at him. In revenge now he has entered this dreidel, to confound the smart guys. Smart guys from Budapest, from Prague, from Cincinnati, even from Vegas.

A dybbuk entering a dreidel? In a Hanukkah toy? Unthinkable you say. Ah, when a soul is angry enough, the demons are released and roam. He blamed the gamblers. They took everything from him. Wife, home, family... life. So now he will take theirs. A dybbuk in a dreidel? Not entirely impossible.

It is seven o'clock in the morning on Thursday. Manny has just pushed the last loser out. For over two days they haven't left their room on the sixth floor of the Stardust. Glasses everywhere. Bottles. Ashtrays full and spilled over. And in two pillowcases, MONEY! Take a guess how much. Two and a half days work for a hot dreidel. Manny counts it while Shelly flops spread-eagled on the bed. He counts a second time. He can't believe it.

"How much did I do?" asks Shelly. Manny says nothing but counts it again. "*Fangoo la matiyana!*" yells Shelly in anger, "How much!"

DREIDEL GOES TO LAS VEGAS...UNBELIEVABLE!

"It's a hundred seventy-four thousand six hundred and eighty-two dollars. Cold cash!"

Shelly lets out a yell like a wild animal. "Shelly Chance. KING KONG OF VEGAS. Out of the forest he came. Unknown. And beat the *kishkes* out of them." Shelly beat his breast like a gorilla. Go, let him try now to climb the outside of the hotel.

"What are you doing, Manny?"

"I'm stuffing the dough into these pillowcases."

"First put the DO NOT DISTURB sign on the door. I don't want any cleaning lady busting in on us," said Shelly.

"Do it yourself," said Manny, "I'm handling the dough."

"I'm the winner. Winners don't put signs on doors. They sent you along to shlep for me. So shlep!" Shelly lay stretched out like a peacock feather at rest.

Manny hung the sign on the door.

"Another thing, Shlep. A pillowcase is no place for big dough. Am I supposed to carry two pillowcases on the airplane? Do something about that, too." ...and Shelly began the peaceful snore of the victorious.

Manny hid the pillowcases under the bed. Then he left to find a fitting carrier for the money. As he walked through the hotel lobby, he sensed that people were staring at him. He felt everyone knew about the money. They knew his secret, that he'd just left in his room pillowcases with nearly two hundred thousand in cash. They would rob him unless he did something quickly.

Manny found two scratched-up leather suitcases in a pawnshop, the kind used to carry dirty underwear to the laundry. In other words, ideal for hiding money.

When he got back to the room it was empty. Empty! He dropped on all fours to look under the bed. The pillowcases were still there. How

DREIDEL GOES TO LAS VEGAS...UNBELIEVABLE!

could Shelly be such a schmuck to leave all the money unguarded? How? Because Shelly woke up hungry. That's how. Manny filled the suitcases with money, holding out eight thousand, which is the only smart thing he did all week. Then he hid the suitcases under a pile of dirty clothes in the closet. That was in the days when hotels had closets. Today they give you a rack, as if to say "Why waste the cost of a door on you? This is good enough." But I digress.

Down in the Stardust Coffee Shop, Shelly was having breakfast at the counter and reading parts of the Chicago Tribune that had been left by a previous tenant. Next to him came and sat down a very large blond lady with lots of curly hair. From what the boys remembered later, I'll try to describe her.

A fuzzy white sweater and around the neck a long thin mink. All over the sweater were designs in sewed-on pearls. On most of her fingers were rings, any of which cost more than I lose in a year. She had dimples and weighed in at a hundred eighty pounds. My Aunt Ernie to a T. Once you see a person like this it shouldn't be hard to spot her again in a crowd, right? Just remember for me that you said yes.

The waitress came and the heavy broad ordered a chocolate milk shake with an egg in it. Plus she handed the waitress an envelope filled with green string. "Please mix this in, Dearie."

Shelly stared at her. How could he help, sitting right next to it?

"Seaweed," said the blonde, "for my complexion." On the counter next to Shelly she set a blue alligator purse, the size of a lawyer's briefcase.

"Would you like some of today's Tribune?" asked Shelly.

The blonde shook her head, no. Every few minutes she started to sniffle. She took from her big purse a fancy handkerchief and touched at the nose and eyes. Then she'd stuff it back in. Shelly watched her do this five or six times. "Why not leave the handkerchief out if she's going to keep using it?" thought Shelly.

DREIDEL GOES TO LAS VEGAS...UNBELIEVABLE!

She couldn't close the purse because it was too full of envelopes and papers, like a desk drawer. On most of the envelopes were names strung together, like the door on a lawyer's office. Was this broad in trouble with the law, wondered Shelly?

"You sure you don't want some of the Trib?" he asked again.

The blonde looked straight at him for a whole minute, absolutely no expression. Just tears leaking out of the corner of her eyes, making black icicles from the mascara. "No, thank you very much," she peeped. A tiny voice came out of her, like from a plastic ocarina. From this big, and I'm not exaggerating, blond came such a small voice. All Shelly could think of was Betty Boop. She looked terrible. Eyes red as tomato juice. "No," she said again in her cute voice. That should have ended it, but Shelly couldn't leave well enough alone. He was after all King Kong.

So they had a conversation, from which Shelly learned three things: a) Her name was Essie, ex-Mrs. Kauffman, b) she was alone here in Vegas, c) her husband Phil Kauffman had just died in a plane crash, which is why the tears. What he didn't learn was d) some planes crash twice.

When Shelly got back to the room, Manny was in the shower. He came out in a towel that didn't reach.

"Where's the dough, Shlep?" asked Shelly.

"Look, my name is Manny. Don't call me Shlep."

"That's what you're here for, to be my shlep. That's the only reason, Shlep. So where's the dough?"

Manny showed him the suitcases, hidden under dirty shirts. "Shelly, let's get outta here."

"Relax. I'm starting to like this town."

"They're watching us. I can feel it. We're going to get stiffed," said Manny.

DREIDEL GOES TO LAS VEGAS...UNBELIEVABLE!

"That's what you're along for. You're my protection." Shelly laughed and patted Manny on the ass.

"This ain't no joke, Shelly. Underneath all the lights and shine, this is a rough town. I feel it. You know we took a lotta dough from those guys."

"Whatareyoutalking? We're chicken feed. Who even notices we won?"

"The guys that lost. They noticed."

"*Fangoo La Matiyana.* They lose big bucks all the time. Millions. They're used to it."

"How's about we get a plane back to Cleveland?"

"We still got two days left on our reservation."

"Screw the reservation. I can change it. Please, Shelly. Let's go," pleaded Manny.

"Look, if we go home now, the syndicate will think we coulda won more if we'd only stayed a couple more days."

"We won enough. You and I agreed to leave if we hit a hundred thousand."

"That was before we hit a hundred seventy-five."

"It's a hundred seventy-four," corrected Manny.

"So? *Fangoo* a thousand."

"Let's go now. We could check out in twenty minutes."

"Look, we stay tonight. Have some fun. A good meal. See a couple shows. Live it up."

Manny paced the room in his towel. "We're gonna lose it all. I can feel it."

"Shut up, Manny. The dough was won fair and square. I bet those guys already got back their losses from a new sucker."

"You think so, Shelly?"

DREIDEL GOES TO LAS VEGAS...UNBELIEVABLE!

"Sure. Relax. These are big boys. They don't cry over spilt milk like Stanley Siegal who gets into a fit when he loses five bucks." Shelly pushed Manny into a chair, "This ain't Cleveland. This is Vegas. What we won is chicken feed."

"You think so?"

"I know so, *Putz*."

"Anyway, I think someone's watching us. That's all."

"The dreidel is watching us. It's saying 'When are we gonna get back to the game'?"

"No, Shelly. No more!" Manny was almost in a panic.

"Relax, *Putz*. The dreidel's in the bag.

That afternoon in the Stardust Dining Room, they were having a late lunch. They had reservations that night for a show with Danny Kaye, plus a magician I never heard of, plus an all-star cast. The tickets alone were twenty bucks, each.

While they were waiting for their steaks to come, who should walk by? In all places, Essie. Shelly introduced her to Manny and asked her to sit down. Which she did "just for a teenie weenie moment," she said in her Betty Boop voice.

Manny shrugged at Shelly, as if to say "What's with this?" Because he normally doesn't pick up such heavy broads.

"I'm sorry about this morning, hon," she said to Shelly. "It's the shock of losing my Phil. Even though we never got along." Again she wiped her eyes.

Before you know it, out comes the whole megillah. Her lawyer is finding insurance policies. Should she sell the apartment building in Miami? Strange people are calling her that she never heard of before. Again the eyes leak. The big purse is set close to Manny.

DREIDEL GOES TO LAS VEGAS...UNBELIEVABLE!

On a paper sticking out he notices some foreign words and numbers. "I notice you're looking at those funny words, hon," she says to Manny. "Do you speak Swiss perhaps?"

Manny shook his head and loosened his collar.

"I think they're numbers of bank accounts. But I'm not sure, hon. Phil used to play around a lot. And he didn't always confide in me." She looked close into Shelly's eyes, eyeball to eyeball. "Don't you think people should trust each other? And tell each other everything?"

"Of course," said Shelly, "you can trust me. You **can trust** Manny."

"Somehow I know I can." She turned to Manny. "**Such** an honest face. Your mother must be proud. It's cold in here, don't you think?" Essie pulled the mink closer around her neck. "Hon, would you please order me a milk shake with an egg." She turned to Manny, "It's for my complexion."

For a moment nobody said anything. But Essie couldn't stand silence. "Manny, you're such a big man. But I bet you call your mother every...." Out of a clear nowhere, the tears welled up and poured out like from a hot shower. "I can't do it! I can't stand it alone! Calls. Calls. Everyone wants from me, God alone knows." More sobbing. She couldn't catch her breath.

"I'm so alone. Shelly, hon, I wish I could find a place to lie down. I don't feel so good. If I could just take the weight off...for a minute." Essie looked like she was going to faint right here.

"We got a room upstairs," said Shelly. Her look of gratitude was the same you'd get from a Golden Retriever puppy.

They led her through the lobby. Only Manny was strong enough to support her weight. Shelly carried her mink and her purse. While they were waiting for the elevator, he gave the inside of her purse another once-over. Metropolitan Life. Equitable. Attorneys Schwartz, Kinder & Block in Miami, plus ten more he didn't have a chance to read. It was true then, Essie was really in the money!

DREIDEL GOES TO LAS VEGAS...UNBELIEVABLE!

When they got her into the room, Manny set her down on the edge of the bed. "Do you mind if I smoke?" Shelly found the gold cigarette case in her purse. She lit up a long Pall Mall. "Let me take my shoes off. My arches are killing me, hon." As she slid off her shoes, the sad tale began again, about strange men calling her. What should she sell? "I know they're stealing from me. But who can I turn to…?" Stuff like that.

Shelly sat down next to her and took her hand. Manny stood near. "I know how it is," Manny said, "When my Aunt Tillie died, she left me those brick apartments in Pittsburgh. I didn't know from nothing about them, but…" Shelly gave him a look to shut up.

Essie took a few puffs. "You two are obviously friends. But I have no one. Who can I turn to? Oh, my girdle is killing me. Who? Who?" Shelly took her handkerchief out of the purse and gave it to her. As she raised her hand to wipe, diamond rings sparkled in the light from the bedlamp. Her sobs were pitiful. Shelly put his arm around her. A welterweight comforting a heavyweight. Bill Kahn and Tony Galento. Essie sobbed herself into exhaustion.

"It feels so good here," she said. "Could I rest awhile?" The tiny Betty Boop voice, tiny as a cricket's. But like a cricket's, you could catch every word. Shelly laid her gently back on the bed and covered her with the folded blanket. Her Pall Mall he took from her limp fingers and put it out in the ashtray. Then he closed the shades and turned out the light.

"Let Essie sleep," he said as he pulled Manny out with him. He locked the door and hung the DO NOT DISTURB sign.

Shelly pulled Manny to the elevator.

"We're leaving her alone?" asked Manny.

"I'm going to marry that broad."

"Essie? What are you talking about? You just met her."

"She's a dame in distress, and I'm going to undistress her."

DREIDEL GOES TO LAS VEGAS...UNBELIEVABLE!

"Look, Shelly, we came out here with a stake from the syndicate. Those guys back home must be getting antsy."

Shelly patted Manny on the cheek. "This is for the syndicate, you *putz*. Essie needs somebody to take care of her and all that dough."

"You?"

"Why not? The syndicate will get a piece of everything I get."

"You're nuts. She ain't gonna marry you. Essie's rich. You saw, she even has money in Swiss. Why would she want to marry a *pisher* like you?"

"Because I got an honest face. She trusts me. Here's the elevator."

They caught a cab and Shelly told the driver to take them to a jewelry store.

"Shelly, don't do this," pleaded Manny.

"Don't do what?"

"Be nice to Essie, that's okay. But don't get tangled with her. You're over your head."

That touched Shelly's pride. "Look, didn't I just fleece the best Vegas has to offer? And with a dreidel no bigger than the end of your *putz*. I can operate in any territory."

"Shelly, don't."

"And I proved it." They sat in silence while the cab waited at this light and that. "How much you got on you?"

Manny lied, "The same five thousand you told me to keep around." He was luckily holding out another three.

"Gimme half for the ring."

"Ring? What ring? Twenty-five hundred for a ring? You gonna stop up a sink with it?" And in those days you could with that kind of money. "It's syndicate money," said Manny. "You can't spend it to buy your broad a ring."

DREIDEL GOES TO LAS VEGAS...UNBELIEVABLE!

"Don't you see, *Putz*, she ain't my broad. She's OUR broad. Everything I get outta this is share and share alike. Except the apartment house in Miami. I'm living there with Essie."

"It ain't right," Manny shook his head in wonderment, "I don't know why, but it ain't right."

Shelly pointed out the cab window. "See those wedding chapels? They ain't there for nothing. They're for me and Essie. And you, *Putz*, will be best man. I'm going to get my Golden Triangle at last!"

"I don't want to be best man."

Of course, Shelly bought the biggest ring he could find. Twenty-seven hundred fifty dollars! But who cares, right? He held it up to the light. "When Essie wakes up, this'll show her how much Shelly loves her."

Outside their hotel room on the sixth floor of the Stardust Hotel, the DO NOT DISTURB sign was still hanging. Shelly knocked softly on the door. A) He didn't want to disturb Essie if she was still knocked out, and B) if she wasn't fully dressed he didn't want to embarrass her before he popped the question.

"A heavy sleeper," Shelly said as he turned the key in the lock.

How can I tell you what comes next without giving you heartburn?

The room was not only empty, it was as if Essie-sobbing-widow-Kauffman had never been there. The bed was neatly made. Not a crease. The blanket neatly folded. Not a blond hair in sight. Where Shelly had put out her Pall Mall, even the ashtray was clean.

Manny ran to the closet. The dirty shirts, she was kind enough to leave. The suitcases? With those she was not so kind. They called the police. Shelly gave a hundred to the Stardust doorman to goose his memory. But nobody saw her! A blond who weighed in at one hundred eighty pounds and nobody saw her! Can you imagine? If the police had just

DREIDEL GOES TO LAS VEGAS...UNBELIEVABLE!

come up with a wrong one. But one! No. For twenty-four hours there was not a blond weighing more than 110 pounds in all of Vegas!

We met them at the Hopkins Airport. Shelly was still cocky but he wasn't the same guy that left. He said the dreidel turned cold on them. And they had a tough time getting up a game.

What happened? What EXACTLY happened? Isn't it natural to question a traveler who has just had your life in his hands? So, one fact trips over another. Manny says this. Shelly says that. Before you know it, out comes the truth. Essie has outwitted us. A woman we've never even met. And when we learn how much, a hundred seventy-four thousand! It's true. The groans of grown men can shatter stones.

We drove immediately to the back of the Texaco. "Tell us again." We wanted every detail. Isn't it amazing how people love to be tortured? At least after the fifth telling, it got easier to take.

Manny was sure Essie was Jewish. Two things. The way she took off her shoes. And how she said his mother must be proud of him. Are these dead giveaways?

Then Phil said, "At least there's a silver lining. All our money didn't go to make a shiksa rich."

For two weeks the moaning went on, you shouldn't be surprised. The what-ifs would have filled a Goodyear blimp. "Oh, bo,y if I had that money now...." I heard it twenty times a day. Miltie Kay had his eye on a dry cleaners. The Blickstein twins always wanted to visit Israel but couldn't afford it. Jake had a line on two racehorses with a desperate owner. Who wouldn't dream things with that kind of money?

When Shelly took the dreidel out of the bag, he noticed a fine crack that wasn't there before. He was ready to go back to Vegas, still sure he could lick it.

Why am I carrying on this way? The story is over. Who cares what might have been? Wait. Don't get up yet. About three weeks later, ten

DREIDEL GOES TO LAS VEGAS...UNBELIEVABLE!

o'clock at night! The phone rings. Long distance. A terrible connection. On the other end a man is asking if I'm part of a syndicate headed by a man named Dreidel.

What is this, I asked myself. How are they coming to me? Of all people? I am being set up, right? So I asked the voice on the phone, "Who is this?"

"Can you put me in touch with Mr. Dreidel?"

Tell me, didn't I have a right to be suspicious?

"It's possible," I say, "Who shall I tell him is calling?"

"This is Mr. Prince. I represent Philip Kauffman. What is Mr. Dreidel's number?"

Philip Kauffman? Do I know such a person? Inside my mind the pointer is racing around. I know a lot of Kauffmans. Which is Philip? Years ago I learned, never admit I know somebody. And never admit I don't' know somebody. You can always remember later, when it's safe. So I asked Mr. Prince, "Is he one of the Cleveland Kauffmans?"

"I'm calling from Miami. It's very important that I reach Mr. Dreidel. It would be worth your while to put me in touch."

Ah hah. He's tightening his own noose. Some lawyer. So I told Mr. Prince that if in the next year or two I ran into Mr. Dreidel, I would certainly mention his call.

That caused agitation. "You don't understand. Mr. Kauffman's wife has been arrested. Mr. Dreidel can clear her."

"For what was she arrested?" I asked.

"I'm not at liberty to say," replied Mr. Prince.

"Then I'm also not at liberty. My regards to Mr. Kauffman." He knew I was about to hang up.

"Wait!" he said.

DREIDEL GOES TO LAS VEGAS...UNBELIEVABLE!

It was dawning on me. "Did your Mr. Kauffman happen to die in a plane crash?"

"No," said the lawyer, "I spoke with him only an hour ago. Then you know him?"

"It must be another Phil Kauffman. From Columbus," I said.

Pulling a little here, and tugging a little there, what story do you think I pried out?

For what was Mrs. Kauffman arrested? Passing counterfeit money! Money she got from a Shelly Dreidel. She sold him a diamond ring to pay off a gambling debt. Some of the money he gave her was counterfeit. That's her story. And now the G-men and Essie are keeping company.

I think to myself, which one was it? Mr. Panama Suit or Pulaski or who? All those people in and out. We'd never know who brought "play money." Or was all of it?

Mr. Prince left me a phone number for Mr. Dreidel to call collect.

Are you starting to weep for Essie already? Be my guest. After I hung up, it dawned on me. My heart was pounding. I was only a breath away from being a convict myself. If Shelly had brought back the money and I had taken my share, how would I know counterfeit from good? Am I a money changer?

I'd have been caught in three minutes. Handcuffs. Fingerprints. All of us would be jailbirds now. So I lost what I never had, but at least I was still free. Which is more than I could say for Essie.

God in Heaven, if I were arrested it would kill my mother, and my father would turn his face away from me in his grave. "For this we raised a good Jewish boy!" she would say and slam the door. It would ring in my ears and be a slice from my heart. Believe me, my heart pounded as if my life hung in the balance. I know I'm not a good person, but bad I'm not either. Once arrested, the case is closed.

DREIDEL GOES TO LAS VEGAS...UNBELIEVABLE!

Strange you say, but for a Jew there really is a point, that I cannot explain, where the line is drawn. One may think evil thoughts, but one does not cross over. Even now my heart beats faster as I retell the story. I and my friends came so close. An angel must have sat on my shoulder. We were saved, but not by our own hand. That idea is repeated so often in our Hebrew prayers. "Rescued by the mighty hand" or "Saved by the goodness of God."

For the ancients, God parted the sea. For us, and I don't speak disrespectful, God took from us tainted money before we could stain our fingers. Is that a miracle? It's okay for me until a better one comes along.

The next day, when I told them in the back of the Texaco, it took a while for some to realize how close the Dark Angel had brushed by.

So what should we do for Mr. Prince?

It was decided that we were sorry, but Mr. Dreidel will be very hard to reach, until he comes back from his Alaskan vacation. As for Essie, they should lock her away in a place where each day she gets a milkshake with an egg for her complexion. However, what if Essie is actually the dybbuk in the dreidel...? in that case, it's a whole 'nother story.

THE DREIDEL DANCER

"YOU HAVE ALREADY WON!" That's what it said on the big brown envelope. An envelope addressed to Shana or Sammy, I can't remember which. From the *"Jewish Sweepstakes!"* "YOU HAVE WON ONE OF THE FOLLOWING FABULOUS PRIZES" said the letter inside. "JUST SEND $15.00 TO COVER POSTAGE AND HANDLING." What were the fabulous prizes? A trip to an Israeli kibbutz that makes cement. Six books of Jewish teenager jokes. One hundred chocolate mezuzahs. On and on. The last prize was an "Indian Dreidel." What was that?

Let me tell you about Shana and Sammy. They were brother and sister, she eleven and he ten. That's easy to believe. What is harder to believe? They got along. Shana didn't throw up at the smell of Sammy's socks left in the bathroom. Sammy didn't deliberately burp in front of her friends. They never fought, except once. At Hanukkah, of all times!

How did it happen? It happened like this. Each year Shana and Sammy would play with a scratched wooden dreidel.

THE DREIDEL DANCER

"Where is it, Ma?"

"In a drawer in the kitchen."

"Where? We can't find it!"

"Look in the toy chest!"

"Where?"…

It took a whole day to find it. Same in your house?

Where were we? Oh yes, the Jewish Sweepstakes. To enter they needed fifteen dollars. Shana and Sammy pooled their allowances and savings and even looked under their beds for lost coins. When it was still not enough, they borrowed five dollars from Father. They sent in the fifteen dollars and waited.

For the next weeks, they ran to the mailbox every day. And every day?—nothing. Late in November UPS came. A box addressed to Sammy or Shana, I can never remember. Inside, wrapped in blue paper, was a lovely dreidel in the shape of a young girl dancer. It was brass, the color of their mother's Sabbath candlesticks. Beautiful! A beautiful dreidel! It shone in the light! Their beautiful new dreidel. Now they wouldn't have to search through drawers for that cheap old, plain old, scratched old, ugly old, wooden dreidel anymore. They never liked it much anyway.

Here was a new golden dreidel! Who got to spin first? I can never remember. Shana said Sammy should spin it. Sammy said Shana should. "After you."

"No, after you." Such kindness! Finally one of them spun the dreidel dancer. What a spin! Leaning this way and that, dipping low, coming upright. For two whole minutes. It spun and spun. Unbelievable! Elated, Sammy and Shana ran to their parents. "You must come and see my dreidel!" said Shana.

"No…It's my dreidel," countered Sammy.

"I was the one who got the sweepstakes letter," said Shana.

THE DREIDEL DANCER

"Oh no you didn't. It was addressed to me!" yelled Sammy.

"Children, children," said Mother calmly. "What are you two arguing about? I thought you wanted to show us something."

Indeed they did. Sammy and Shana led their parents to the table where Dreidel Dancer lay resting.

"Ta Da!" they both exclaimed.

"Ta Da, what?" asked Father. "What's the big deal?"

"What's the big deal? We'll show you," said Sammy.

"Go ahead, Mom, spin it," said Shana.

Mother gave it a gentle spin. This time, as it was spinning, it spelled out M-O-M. Then it slowly fell and lay at rest.

"See!" said Shana, "Isn't it a wonderful dreidel?"

Everyone applauded, Shana, Sammy, Mom and Dad. The Dreidel Dancer, though no one touched it, gave the slightest rocking motion, as if to say "Thank you."

After dinner the children tried playing with it again. For some reason, it wouldn't spin. It just fell over. Shana saw tarnish marks on the side …from handling the shiny brass. She got out the polish that Mother used to clean the Sabbath candlesticks. Shana polished Dreidel Dancer. It shone brilliantly in the lamplight. Shana picked up Dreidel Dancer and tried spinning it again. It spun wonderfully. Even better than before.

"Do you think it just wanted to be polished?" asked Sammy.

"Maybe it doesn't want to spin unless it looks pretty," said Shana.

"What a smart dreidel. Won't spin unless it looks beautiful."

And that was true. If Dreidel Dancer got the least bit tarnished, you couldn't make it spin.

Shana felt it was her duty to keep Dreidel Dancer polished. EVERY DAY. Even if she didn't have time to finish her homework.

THE DREIDEL DANCER

So Shana felt perfectly justified taking it to temple the first night of Hanukkah, and showing it off.

Sammy was very upset. "That's my dreidel. You had no right to take it without asking me!"

"Your dreidel!" replied Shana in a huff. "Do you spend hours polishing it? No. You just want to spin it and do none of the work."

"I'd polish if I had the chance. But no, you always hide it in your room!" yelled Sammy.

Once Dreidel Dancer was shown at temple, word spread fast. This dreidel seemed to be alive. It danced like a real person. Children couldn't believe their eyes. Mother was so impressed with Dreidel Dancer, she sewed a carrying bag out of a scrap of expensive imported silk. Temple parents called Mother. Was the story their children brought home true? "Of course, it's true. Dreidel Dancer is something to behold."

It didn't take long for Channel 3, the local TV station, to call for an interview. But only if Dreidel Dancer would do tricks. LIVE. The afternoon of the TV show, Shana polished and polished. She spent so much time, she lost track of it. It was past the time to leave for the 6 o'clock news show. They hurried to the station.

Waiting in the TV studio guest room, Sammy tried spinning Dreidel Dancer to make sure everything was okay. It wasn't. It just flopped over. My goodness! What had gone wrong? They were due on the air in fifteen minutes! The bag! The silk carrying bag their mother had made. Shana had left it home. That must be it. Dreidel Dancer wanted to be carried into the TV studio in that elegant silk bag. Sammy ran home as fast as he could. Luckily Father was just coming from work. He drove Sammy back to the studio. Now it was only minutes before they were due on the air. Sammy rushed in with the bag. Shana put the dreidel inside. They went into the studio. When the Director saw Sammy, all

THE DREIDEL DANCER

sweaty from running, he said that would never do. Sammy would have to wait outside. Sammy was crushed; some deal, after he'd run all the way home! Shana was excited. She was going to be on TV! Would she remember to smile, as Mother told her?

She needn't have worried. The TV cameras never pointed at her. Only at Dreidel Dancer, who performed perfectly. It even gave a little hop in the middle of the spin, something the children had never seen it do before. Dreidel Dancer was a great success. The dreidel segment was picked up by the CBS network. People everywhere saw Dreidel Dancer. Fan mail started coming in. Nearly forty letters the first week.

A widow from Akron, Ohio named Mrs. Cheryl Beasley was so taken with Dreidel Dancer she sent a jeweled carrying case. It had real rubies and opals on the outside and mirrors all over the inside. Mrs. Beasley wrote a letter along with the case that said she appreciated the finer things in life now that her husband had passed away. And she thought Dreidel Dancer was one of those things.

When Dreidel Dancer was laid inside, it gave that slight rocking motion which the children recognized as the Dreidel's way of saying "thank you." They soon found that Dreidel Dancer wouldn't spin unless it was carried around in the jeweled case.

Fan mail continued to arrive in huge bundles. The phone rang constantly. It was hectic. One morning, when things were in total chaos, there was a knock at the door. Mr. Oylie Oxford, entertainment agent, appeared. He wore a black cashmere sport coat, a yellow vest, and grey spats. I'll make you RICH!" he promised, "I ABSOLUTELY believe that." But only if they followed his suggestions.

After all, he'd made the Seven Golden Parakeets, who sang grand opera, famous. They knew about that, didn't they? No? At any rate, Oylie said he was famous for making fortunes for others, and he'd do the same for this family. In fact, if they could come to an agreement this afternoon, he'd practically guarantee an appearance on David Letterman's show within six weeks.

"You'd better be smiling when the spotlight goes on! Because Oylie Oxford is famous for getting things done."

The family agreed. What other choice did they have? They knew nothing about show business. In the days that followed, Oylie Oxford was as good as his word. Things got organized: Dreidel Dancer had many public appearances, opening a Ford dealer's tent sale and two new courthouses. It even opened a shopping mall in South Bend! A Hebrew dreidel in the hometown of Notre Dame! Oylie would only let it travel by private limo. Dreidel Dancer rode alone in the jeweled case on the back seat. "Gives it some class," said Oylie. If Sammy or Shana wanted to go along, they had to sit up front with the driver.

A professional jewelry polisher was hired, to make sure Dreidel Dancer had a *perfect* shine. Shana, of course, was only an amateur shiner. Oylie Oxford arranged for the donation of a white Siberian mink wrap, from the Polenski Mink Growers Cooperative, a newly-formed capitalistic company in east Siberia. He told a USA Today reporter, "this is another example of *glasnost, perestroika* and the indomitable human spirit."

After that Dreidel Dancer wouldn't perform unless first wrapped in white mink from Polenski's Mink Cooperative. Mother's silk carrying bag was abandoned and forgotten in one of the crowded kitchen drawers. Because Dreidel Dancer was so valuable, a beefy Brinks guard was hired to watch it. Naturally, Dreidel Dancer refused to perform unless it had a full morning's rest. The house had to be ABSOLUTELY quiet. *No personal appearances before noon* was the standing rule. Only reluctantly would it spin for Shana or Sammy. A large audience and/or a spotlight were now minimum requirements.

Every week the widow, Mrs. Beasley, called from Akron to find out why Dreidel Dancer hadn't been on the Oprah show yet. Oylie Oxford

THE DREIDEL DANCER

assigned Shana and Sammy important jobs—answering fan mail. Bags and piles were stacked in every open space in the house. The children spent all their free time answering fan mail. They addressed envelopes and stuffed *signed* color photos of Dreidel Dancer inside.

Although Dreidel Dancer was being paid large fees for personal appearances, nothing was left at the end of each month. There were so many expenses. The limo, the Brinks' guard, Oylie Oxford's fees, the cost of *signed* color photos, postage, a professional jewelry polisher, long distance calls, travel expenses…the list was endless.

"Don't worry," said Oylie Oxford, "things are snowballing. Absolutely I believe, within a year you'll all be rich!"

"So what?" said Sammy, addressing his 214th fan envelope of the day.

"Yeh, so what?" said Shana, addressing her 258th fan envelope of the day.

Oylie couldn't help sensing their frustration. He told Shana and Sammy he was going to set aside $10 for every hour they worked on fan mail. It would go into a college fund so they'd never have to worry about getting a scholarship.

"Big deal," said Shana.

"Likewise," said Sammy.

Who'd have dreamed their lovely Dreidel Dancer could cause such frustration?

Then Oylie announced, "Great news. We've got a spot on David Letterman's show!"

Oylie and Dreidel Dancer flew first class out to New York. The jeweled case with Dreidel Dancer inside had a seat of its own. Sammy and Shana were invited to go along, but they had to sit in Coach to save money. Nonetheless, it was a thrill.

The night of the show, Oylie ordered the children to check everything:

THE DREIDEL DANCER

Was it polished? Check.

Was it wrapped in the white mink? Check.

Had it rested till noon? Check.

Was it still in the jeweled carrying case? Check.

David Letterman treated Dreidel Dancer like a big joke. As if it were a dog that pranced around on its hind legs.

The dreidel was shining in the bright lights, lying on the white mink wrap. It seemed to be quivering.

Letterman made a joke. "Why, the thing actually looks nervous." The audience giggled.

To a drum roll, Letterman picked up Dreidel Dancer. "So this is your above-average performing dridela?" He deliberately mispronounced "dreidel." That got a big laugh. Letterman gave it a spin.

Shana and Sammy were on the edge of their seats. Had they forgotten anything? Would the dreidel spin or decide to fall over and make fools of them all?

It spun. Did it spin! …and spin and spin, moving around the top of David Letterman's desk. It carefully spun around papers, pens, glasses… around all the objects on his desk, as if it could SEE. Letterman waited for Dreidel Dancer to run out of steam. But it didn't drop. It just kept spinning.

"Well, folks, we've got to go to a commercial break… but we'll be right back to see the conclusion of the incredible spinning dridela."

They broke for commercials about the incredible smoothness of a Gillette shave, and the incredible smoothness of Coors Lite. When they cut back to Letterman, Dreidel Dancer was still spinning, with incredible smoothness. David was flummoxed. Should he introduce the next guest and ignore the dreidel? I mean, a spinning dreidel can get pretty boring.

THE DREIDEL DANCER

But a few rowdies in the studio audience had taken up a dreidel chant. They were calling out the seconds Dreidel Dancer had been spinning... 489, 490, 491. The drummer hit the cymbals every ten seconds. Those who weren't counting started clapping. Letterman lost control. The audience had taken over. He had a sheepish grin on his face. You could see a stalled tongue through the big gap in his front teeth.

The director mercifully cut to another commercial break. Dreidel Dancer spun through three commercial breaks. When they came back to Letterman the fourth time, the audience was up to... 877, 878, 879.

Four stagehands started to carry Letterman's desk out of the studio with Dreidel Dancer still spinning on top. But the dreidel was too clever for them. Still spinning, it leaped to the floor, then climbed up the wall of windows behind Letterman's desk, up to the raft of pipes holding the studio lights. The cameras panned up, but lost dreidel in the glare. The audience was going wild... 921, 922, 923, clapping and stamping their feet.

Next, Dreidel Dancer came down the far wall behind the band. It spun across Paul Shaffer's feet and to the spot where Letterman's desk had been. He was standing on a chair, like someone afraid of a mouse.

In front of Letterman's chair, the dreidel leaped in the air and did three complete loops. Then it spun in an ever smaller circle, like a champion ice skater, spinning faster and faster. Finally, it performed a slow layout and came to rest.

The clapping and cheering lasted at least five minutes. Letterman joined in when he regained his cool.

Oylie Oxford turned red with excitement. "UNBELIEVABLE. UNBELIEVABLE. THIS THING IS GOING STRATOSPHERIC."

Shana took Sammy's hand. No one paid any attention to them. You can imagine how they felt. Their dreidel had wowed the country on

THE DREIDEL DANCER

national TV. But it was Oylie Oxford who did the on-camera interview. He told the two children that as a professional, he knew best how to handle the press. Because a trip to the White House was now in the cards.

It certainly was an exciting year for Dreidel Dancer. Home life was something else. Father couldn't sit anywhere to read his paper in peace. Mother could never get the kitchen clean. The beefy **Brinks guard** was forever raiding the refrigerator. Sammy and Shana **started** cutting school to keep up with the fan mail. And the phone rang **constant**ly for Oylie Oxford.

The week before Hanukkah, Shana and Sammy thought it would be fun to play with a dreidel. Naturally, they'd never dream of playing with the beautiful, famous Dreidel Dancer. First of all, who wants to play dreidel with a beefy Brinks guard standing over you? And Dreidel Dancer might not spin if it was resting or getting ready for a grand opening or a parade or something.

On Tuesday morning, the day before Hanukkah, Oylie Oxford called the whole family together.

"Believe me, I know how this disrupts your family," he said. "The phone calls for me. I don't know why they don't use my office phone."

"I thought you disconnected that to save money?" Shana chimed in.

"Yes. No. Kid, that's not the point," said Oylie Oxford, "all this isn't fair. You should be enjoying the money." He quickly remembered there hadn't been any money for them to enjoy. "There will be. There will be!"

"Yah, I'll be sixty-eight years old then," cracked Sammy.

"Don't be smart, Sammy," said Mother, "Mr. Oxford is working very hard for all of us, aren't you Mr. Oxford?"

"I am? Oh, I am. Listen. I've absolutely an idea. What if I took the Dreidel Dancer and the jewel box over to my office? I'll reconnect the phone. That way you can all live in peace again."

THE DREIDEL DANCER

Mother said, "Oh, if you wouldn't mind, Mr. Oxford."

And that's how it happened. They seldom saw Dreidel Dancer again, except on TV and in the color pictures they were sending to the fans. The first night of Ḥanukkah, Shana and Sammy searched through the kitchen drawers for their old dreidel. At the back of the scarf and mitten drawer, they found it. Their old wooden dreidel. They hadn't seen it in nearly two years. It looked so…what's the word? …comfortable. They spun it. *Shin. Gimmel, Hay. Nun.* "I had a little dreidel, they made it out of wood. It dropped for me a *Gimmel*, that's just the way it should."

What fun they had…then.

And when they'd finished, Shana put the old wooden dreidel in the beautiful silk bag Mother had made.

DREIDEL STOPS HERE/AMTRAK DOESN'T

In Michigan are two small cities, maybe twenty miles apart. In each is a Reform Jewish congregation. One has money, but no building. The other has a building, and no money. Give you an idea?

The names of these congregations? To protect their privacy, let's call them after their presidents. The one with the building, we'll call Congregation "Schaffer," after President Sid Schaffer, a scrap dealer. The one with money, we'll call Congregation "Block," after President Tillie Block, the full-bosomed mother image.

Our story begins. Where?

President Tillie Block was holding a monthly temple board meeting in her apartment. After old business, she was handed a letter by board treasurer Mort Firestein. Tillie opened the letter. It's from the Building and Supplies Committee of Third Methodist Church. Third Methodist

DREIDEL STOPS HERE/AMTRAK DOESN'T

is Congregation Block's landlord. This is the one, you remember, without a building. She scanned the contents before reading aloud, but as she read to herself, a vibrant reddish glow appeared above her ruffled pink blouse, and spread up to her face.

She flung the letter back to Mort, the treasurer. "I've never been so insulted in my life. You read it, Mort. As president, I don't have to take this kind of abuse."

Mort looked around. What should he do?

Trustee Jerry Albert grabbed the letter. "Come on, come on," said Jerry. What's the big deal? I'll read it"…and so he did.

> *Dear Temple Board:*
>
> *It has come to the attention of our Supplies Committee that an excessive amount of toilet paper is being used, approximately 17% more than in prior years. (A graph showing the use of toilet paper on a monthly basis for the last five years is attached.)*
>
> *Also, from time to time certain water faucets are left in a dripping mode.*
>
> *Although we are pleased to rent space to your Congregation for your Friday night services, and for other special days in your Hebrew Religious Calendar, our budgetary limits mean we need to watch costs at every opportunity.*
>
> *You can agree these are difficult financial times. We appreciate your cooperation in this delicate matter, and trust that you will see that excessive amounts of toilet paper will not be used. Please also ensure that water faucets will be left in a non-drip, off-mode on exiting the kitchen or restrooms. Perhaps you could make several announcements to this effect during your services.*

DREIDEL STOPS HERE/AMTRAK DOESN'T

In the spirit of cooperation, we are sending a similar letter to other groups renting the Church's facilities. We want to assure you that Jewish persons are not being singled out for special treatment.

In closing, we appreciate your understanding.

Yours in Christ,

John M. Sebring, Chm
Building and Finance Committee

For a moment, no one spoke. They fumed, but didn't speak.

Finally Mort, the teasurer, burst out, "What kind of cockamaimie letter is this? There are three other groups meeting in their building on Friday nights. The Natural Food Collective, Single Parents and Silent Partners, and the Divorcee Federation. But we get blamed!"

Trustee Jerry chimed in, "What do they think? We hold services in the bathrooms? We need their water? What are we, Jewish Baptists…or what?" Jerry slapped his hand on the table. "We should have our own building. Then we wouldn't have to take this stuff."

"No, no, no, absolutely not," Treasurer Mort waved his arms. "You think too much toilet paper is something? If we owned the building year-round, every nickel-dime thing we'd worry about."

Tillie said, "Much as I'd love our own building, with only forty-nine member families, what kind of place could we support? Each year Hebrew Union College demands more money for our student rabbis. Ronny Landsman is a charming boy. But when we raised our dues again this year to pay the extra, my phone rang off the hook!"

"Just the same," said Jerry, "if we had our own building, members could see their money going for something. And we wouldn't have to take this."

…thus Tillie's board meeting went merrily along.…

DREIDEL STOPS HERE/AMTRAK DOESN'T

You may find this too much of a coincidence, but another temple board meeting was going on at this very moment 20 miles away…in the home of President Sid Schaffer.

Sid's wife, Rosalie, eavesdropped. Another argument was about to begin between Fred Nash, Treasurer, and Ben Wallenstein, Vice President. The subject? *The Fast-Deteriorating Condition of the Temple Building.*

Vice President Ben said, "You wouldn't believe what I went through! Last Friday night, I bring a new couple to services, Henry Winter, a dentist, and his wife, from an important family in Toledo. What happens? We come into the sanctuary and here are buckets, catching drips from the ceiling! How does that look, Fred!"

"Money grows on trees? Is that what you think?" Fred yelled right back at him.

"Don't change the subject. Tell me how it looks!"

President Sid tried to intervene. "Gentlemen, please, this isn't something we should argue about now. Sheila, our student rabbi, will be here any minute. You want her to see us behaving like crazy men? Calm down."

Ben wouldn't. "I'll calm down when he tells me how it looks, dammit! I'm bringing in a potential member family, and we trip over a bucket in the sanctuary? Water! In a bucket! What are we, Baptists or something?"

"What he means, Fred…," started Sid.

"I know what he means," said Fred. "What does he expect? I'm going to reach into my pocket to get his roof fixed? Twenty-one thousand dollars! Where's it coming from? Ask him that. You're the president!"

But Sid didn't know. "Fred, You're the treasurer. You know where the funds are. Our endowment fund. There's money in there."

Absolutely not," said Fred. "You can't touch endowment. It's for a rainy day."

DREIDEL STOPS HERE/AMTRAK DOESN'T

"Fred, this is a rainy day," said Sid, "When I sit up on the *bima* and the water is dripping on the leather chair next to me, who knows when it will drip on my head? A Noah I'm not."

Fred folded his arms, like a banker about to turn down a loan. "Wake up, my friends. Money is going out faster than it's coming in. You can't keep up a building, pay a student rabbi to fly in twice a month from Cincinnati, first class yet, print parchment announcements for High Holy Days, get the grass cut, the snow shoveled for free. It's got to be paid for. And thirty-six active member families aren't exactly a pot of gold, my friends." He rested his case.

Impasse? No. Because another issue should have been raised—should have been raised months ago. Ben Wallenstein decided now was the time. "You think the doctors still want to buy our building?"

"For their clinic?" asked Fred.

"Who else? They've been hounding us for three years. And they're talking cash."

President Sid stood in an approximately upright position. His back hurt from sitting too long. "I will not be the president under whose term this congregation sells its birthright for a mess of pottage. This building has been our temple for sixty-three years."

Ben said, "Sid, is it your fault the roof leaks? Is it your fault the boiler is giving out? Is it your fault the foundation's cracked? Your fault?"

"So Sid," said Fred, "Who's got money to fix all those things? Who, I ask? You? Only doctors have that kind of money, Sid. Only doctors."

"Think about it, Sid," said Ben. The site alone is worth twenty times what we paid for it. We're sitting on a choice commercial location. Does a Reform Jewish temple need a choice commercial location? Of course not."

Sid stood thoughtfully. He couldn't make up his mind. "So you think it's right, Fred? You're the treasurer."

DREIDEL STOPS HERE/AMTRAK DOESN'T

Fred stretched. "It would be a great weight off my shoulders. In the meantime, we could rent space from a church, temporarily. Like Congregation Block, only twenty miles away."

"I am informed confidentially, they get along beautifully with that church. They are very happy with the relationship. Their membership is growing, which is more than I can say for ours."

Eyes turned to Sid. Well? He dreaded deciding. A heavenly messenger saved him. The doorbell chimed.

"That must be our student rabbi, Sheila. She wants to meet us about some ideas for Rosh ha-Shanah. What a wonderful, bright girl. She knows nothing about our building problem. Nothing about our budget problem. So please, Fred, Ben, not a word."

The doorbell chimed again. "Rosalie, dear, please. The front door."

"Yes, Sidney, darling." Rosalie had been listening from the kitchen. Later she would have words with the president.

Student Rabbi Sheila Bronfman walked briskly into the room, handed her coat to Rosalie. She shook hands firmly all around and sat. "I'd like to talk with you first about the leaking roof in the sanctuary...."

AH HAH!

Now that you understand the problem with these two congregations, let's meet an angel. A meddling angel.

Harold Ginsburg, rich man. A retired pharmacist who sold a chain of drugstores. Now he has money, to meddle. As a giver to many Jewish causes, Ginsburg has contacts in both congregations.

An inner voice said, "Harold. There are two fine Jewish congregations on the brink. So do something." He did. He called his friendly attorney, Phil Pincus. "Phil, I need a favor."

"A favor from me? Attorneys don't do favors. They do fees."

DREIDEL STOPS HERE/AMTRAK DOESN'T

Ginsburg asked, "You still have the property where your apartments burned down?

"You mean the property in Murphysville?" asked Pincus.

"That's the one."

"The price just went up a hundred thousand. What do you want with it?"

"The two congregations are having trouble. Congregation Block needs a building and Congregation Schaffer needs money.

"Ginsburg, you've got bum information, Congregation Schaffer must be sitting on a pile of cash. One of my clients has been trying to buy their building. Offered them twice what it's worth. Couldn't budge 'em."

"I heard different," said Harold. "Anyway, I'm going to do a little matchmaking, and I need you for a dowry."

The town of Murphysville? What's an Irish name doing in a Jewish story? These congregations are twenty miles apart, right? That doesn't mean there's no life in between. In between is a small village started by an Irish potato farmer, Murphy. No Jews live in Murphysville. It's even too small for Amtrak to stop. But it does have a beautiful little river running through. On the banks of the river, Pincus owns now-vacant property.

A week later, Harold Ginsburg had lunch with Tillie Block. Casually, he mentioned that certain people had approached him about heading a building fund for Congregation Block. What did she think?

"Harold, who needs the headaches of a building when things are going so well with the Methodist Church?"

"If they are, you don't. I heard otherwise, Tillie."

"Harold, you know. People talk."

"Congregation Schaffer, and this is strictly confidential, Tillie, is considering building somewhere else. Out of downtown. You two... twenty miles apart... I thought it would be interesting to explore."

53

DREIDEL STOPS HERE/AMTRAK DOESN'T

"Well, I don't know, Harold. They always seemed so standoffish. Personally, I got along fine. But… strictly confidential… they put on airs, Harold. They had a building and we didn't."

"I see. Well, that's too bad.…"

"What exactly did you have in mind? What did you mean…explore'?"

"Explore, you know, socially. Hanukkah is coming in two months. Maybe a joint service. You each have a student rabbi. They could get together and plan something… just an idea.…"

"Of course, I'd have to consult my board."

"Of course."

So he had one "Yes."

A few days later, Harold went to see President Sid at his scrapyard. Sid ran the family scrap business in a white shirt every day and never a dirty fingernail. The two men talked. Sid agreed to bring it before his board. He could see no harm in a joint service. After all, Jews should be friendly with each other, if at all possible. In a week, Ginsburg had "Yes" answers from both Boards. He'd have to work fast. Late October. Hanukkah was only seven weeks away.

Two "Yeses." A miracle appropriate for Hanukkah. Fine. But which congregation would host the joint service? Quite an honor, you understand. Jealousies are possible. So clever Ginsburg came up with an unbiased way of choosing. Spin a dreidel. Hanukkah! Why not?

He called Tillie on the phone, explaining the problem of choosing a host congregation. "Tillie, you got a dreidel in the house? Get it. Spin it and tell me what letter comes up."

She did. The Hebrew letter was shin. "Congratulations. You win. You're the host Congregation!"

Tillie was thrilled. "I've got to make plans! But Harold, what should we do? You know, they have a reputation for being critical and standoffish."

DREIDEL STOPS HERE/AMTRAK DOESN'T

"Do what you usually do. Have everyone bring a family menorah for candle-lighting. Make latkes. Pour the Manischewitz. Loosen people up. Have games for the children. Write this down. Eight o'clock, Friday night. Second night of Hanukkah. Tell the Rabbis to get together and plan a service."

"Should I contact Sid and tell him the news?"

"No," Ginsburg said, "Leave that to me. It will be my pleasure."

He called Sid at home, giving the same explanation and sending Sid looking for a Dreidel. "Spin it and tell me what letter comes up."

"*Gimmel.* Is that good?"

"*Gimmel* is great, Sid. Congratulations. You're the host congregation."

"Now what should I do?" asked a bewildered Sid. "Rosalie, get on the phone."

"Start making plans," said Ginsburg. "Have everyone bring a family menorah for candle-lighting. Make latkes." All the things he told Tillie, he told Sid. "Write this down. Eight o'clock, Friday night. Second night of Hanukkah." Both Congregations are host? What's going on?

Far away, in Cincinnati, at Hebrew Union College where Ronny and Sheila were studying for the rabbinate, they met outside the library. It would be hard to find more opposite peas in the same pod. Sheila was tall, with glistening black hair. A girl people knew was brilliant from the time she was two. Ronny was shorter, less assured. Ronny Landsman *felt* his Judaism. For him, folk music was liturgy of the heart. Singing. Clapping. Stamping feet. "Hello, God." On the other hand, Sheila Bronfman was hewn from the rock of intellect. She knew there was "one way" to run services. A Rabbi must bring Dignity to Worship.

Because their congregations requested it, they were honor-bound to get up a joint service. But what? What could they do special? Ronny suggested a story about Hanukkah in Helm, the village of the foolish. Sheila said she'd been outlining a sermon comparing the Maccabees

DREIDEL STOPS HERE/AMTRAK DOESN'T

with Islamic fundamentalists in Iran. Current and appropriate for Hanukkah.

"Doesn't sound very festive," said Ronny.

"Does everything have to be festive? This is Judaism, not a circus!"

Of course.

Finally, it was Friday night, second night of Hanukkah, 8 o'clock. Most members of Congregation Schaffer were gathered in their building. Thank heavens it wasn't raining. A welcome banner was hung across the Social Hall. Families had brought in their menorahs to light up during services. Sheila Bronfman was resplendent in blue robe and a white prayer shawl embroidered by her mother, and a speech of conviction lay folded on the pulpit. After her talk with Ronny, she softened the punch. But her unusual comparison of the Maccabees and the Islamic fundamentalists was left in. Sheila believed a true religious leader lets the chips fall where they may. The people waited for their fellow Jews from Congregation Block. Who didn't show at the appointed hour. Or even fifteen minutes past the appointed hour. No one showed up! Sid was a nervous wreck. Everyone blamed him. It was his stupid plan!

In a city twenty miles away it was also 8 p.m. on the second night of Hanukkah. Members of Congregation Block were gathered in the big social room of the Methodist Church. It had been reserved for the Divorcees Dance. But Mort Firestein offered them three hundred dollars, or to rent the F.O.E. hall for them. It was bigger, nicer and had plenty of parking. The Divorcees took the hall *and* kept Mort's three hundred dollars. They were used to dealing with alimony.

Ronny Landsman had prepared a Hassidic tale for his sermon, a bit more romantic and dignified than a Helm story.

By twelve minutes after eight still no one had appeared from Congregation Schaffer. Tillie was livid. "I never felt good about this affair. Those people are so cliquish."

DREIDEL STOPS HERE/AMTRAK DOESN'T

A phone call came for Tillie. It was from Harold Ginsburg. "Tillie, my love, there's been a terrible mistake. It's my fault. I think I confused the Schaffer people. They thought the joint service was at their building."

"Tell the truth, Harold. Those people don't want to join us in a simple service, just because it wasn't at their building!"

"Tillie, I take full responsibility. I've chartered a Greyhound to drive you, so as not to inconvenience anybody. It's parked in the church lot, right outside your door. Have people take along your decorations, menorahs, latkes, a few prayerbooks and whatever else and get on the bus."

"Harold, you must be joking. Our congregation on a Greyhound? What do you think we are, a football team going to Indiana?"

"Tillie, please. Do as I say. It will all work out."

A few minutes later the phone rang at Congregation Schaffer. President Sid was called to the phone.

"Sid, this is Harold Ginsburg. I've made a terrible mistake. I must have confused Congregation Block. they think services are going to be held at their place. You can understand, everything at the last minute. The confusion and all."

Sid was upset. "There was no confusion. Tell the truth, Harold. Those people just don't want to join us in a simple service."

"You're wrong. You're wrong, Sid. I assure you. It's my fault. Look, not to inconvenience you, I've chartered a Greyhound. It's in your parking lot right now. Just move your congregation in. Take your decorations, menorahs, latkes...."

"A Greyhound bus?" said Sid. "Are we going to Indiana?"

Of course, they got on the buses. What choice did they have? People were confused. "What's going on?" "Whose idea was this?"

Once on the buses, they found that Ginsburg had prepared hot knishes, honey cakes, coffee, hot chocolate. All in all, if not a feast, not

DREIDEL STOPS HERE/AMTRAK DOESN'T

bad on a cold night in Michigan. Are these congregations playing musical temples? We said that between these cities is a village called Murphysville. Would you believe, both buses ran out of fuel going through that village, from opposite directions? They had to send for AAA to bring diesel. It would take an hour.

But Greyhound buses don't run out of fuel. A miracle? The buses just made it to the parking lot of an old Farmer's Grange Hall. Ginsburg happened to know where a key was hidden. A hundred-year-old building in perfect shape. Wooden floors, a stage for the *bima*, and plenty of folding chairs. There was even a kitchen downstairs to warm up the latkes and apple sauce. And the heat had been turned on. What more could you ask for on a cold December night? **A Miracle?**

People piled out of the buses. What are we doing in the middle of nowhere? Like the children of Israel again, wandering in the desert to a place even Amtrak doesn't stop. Plenty of questions were asked, but none answered. Ginsburg played dumb. People were upset, sure. But in no time spirits changed. The old hall was so charming. Several historians in both congregations admired the workmanship. Old Grange awards hung in dusty gilt frames. A small group of preservationists discussed a petition to the governor.

On the stage, the service began. Two sitting presidents. Two student rabbis. And the roof didn't leak.

How did it go, the joint service? Wonderful! The first time in either congregation, that responsive reading wasn't mumbled. It shook the walls. People joined in the singing Ronny led. Not one, but three songs before they were satisfied to go on. The story Ronny told, of a poor Hassidic student who couldn't afford candles for his Hanukkah menorah, brought a few wet eyes around. At that moment, all the children came forward with their menorahs for a grand lighting of the second night's candles. Electric lights were turned off and the rest of the service was held by candlelight.

DREIDEL STOPS HERE/AMTRAK DOESN'T

Yes, Sheila did her sermon, too. But it was different than what she'd written. She spoke of the memories of her girlhood. Her whole family, cousins and uncles she'd never met, getting together for her oldest sister's wedding. From far and wide. "When people as Jews gather like this, from wherever they come, and however simple the place, the glow that happens creates a new star here," she said. "And this place becomes the center of another universe." Such romantic thoughts from Sheila were certainly a miracle.

Ronny and Sheila led the singing of *Maoz Tzur*, the closing hymn. Rock of Ages. And then it was latke time. At the end, warm, refueled buses took everyone home.

What was the result? In the days that followed, people talked excitedly about a joint congregation. After all, why should Jews that live only twenty miles apart be so standoffish from each other? Congregation Schaffer expressed a willingness to sell their building and donate the proceeds to a common temple. Congregation Block was willing to donate their large endowment fund to the new cause. A joint building committee was formed to talk seriously.

Ginsburg planted a strong rumor. Attorney Pincus might donate his parcel on the river in Murphysville for the new Temple. Sounds great! You think the story is over? Not quite. Life isn't a story. Plans that ought to go well turn to smoke. Why? Human beings.

So what was the hold-up? Who was to be the rabbi of the new congregation—that was the hold-up. "Unless our dear Ronny is the new Rabbi, I won't give a red cent."

One side said, "Your rabbi is a kid. Lacks maturity."

The other said, "Your rabbi isn't religious enough." And so forth and so forth.

Noise. Static. No one knew if the cacklers were a majority or not. Ginsburg suggested a joint board meeting. Both temples, before every-

DREIDEL STOPS HERE/AMTRAK DOESN'T

thing fell apart. At Tillie's apartment. What happened? President Sid read a statement signed by thirty-two members of his Congregation, and seven members from Tillie's.

> "RESOLVED: We support in principle the choice of a female rabbi for our new congregation. It and she symbolize for us a dramatic departure from the past, a new beginning for Reform Judaism...."

You can make up the rest.

Tillie stood up from her chair, her ample bosom heaving with emotion. "I admit that Ronny has been like a son to me," Tillie began. "For me it is hard to accept a total stranger. Yes, Sheila's a scholar. And I agree someday she will be an important Jewish figure. But recall it **was** Ronny's simple *mazel*, his music which drew us all together that fateful...."

It got worse.

"Only Ronny."

"Only Sheila."

"You were always pig-headed, Fred, in a kosher way."

"Max, it's as plain as the nose on your ugly face."

"Absolutely."

"Positively."

"My final position."

"My last word."

Then the phone rang. It rang insistently. Tillie picked it up.

"Hello. Yes, dear," she said, her eyes lighting up, "Oh, how nice." A long pause. The rosy color in her face vanished. "How wonderful. Yes, it is quite a surprise. But do you think you're making the right decision?" She listened and nodded and nodded and listened. But said nothing.

DREIDEL STOPS HERE/AMTRAK DOESN'T

Finally, in the saddest voice you could imagine, Tillie said, "*Mazel tov*," and hung up.

She turned to her fellow board members. "It seems congratulations are in order. Ronny and Sheila are engaged. Ronny said our goodness brought them together. They think we're such sharing people, both congregations. Giving. Not dogmatic. They were hired as a team by a temple in Knoxville. So how do you like that? She sat like a bushel of potatoes.

"That's *all* he said?" Fred asked.

"No. Ronnie said it will be easy for us to find another rabbi. We're famous at Hebrew Union in Cincinnati. We are considered adventurous."

So you see, don't count your chickens too early.

Everything is not in our control. Some things just happen. Look at the stars. Do they care? If they don't care and they've been around longer than us why should we get so upset?

Well, it was on the Paul Harvey news, about two small congregations joining forces, and the rabbis from each getting married and going to Tennessee. Paul Harvey was not a favorite person with some members of the building committee. What business was it of his?

But for a time, at least, arguing was out of fashion. Another miracle? The greatest miracle, though, was that a Jewish congregation got started in a town with no Jews—a town so small, even Amtrak doesn't stop.

MARK OF THE DREIDEL

Bernie Kinsman decided he could stand it no longer. An ultimatum was due. Today. No more Mr. Nice Guy.

Lily and Rose, his sisters-in-law, would have to go. The living situation was driving him nuts. One man in a household of five females! Lily and Rose, his wife Peg the beauty, and his two little girls, Sissie and Penny. Could you stand such a thing? It wouldn't be easy, he knew that. He'd have to pay all the rent on the apartment. All. Nearly $200 a month. Two hundred dollars is a lot? Think of a time over sixty years ago, when your grandfather was still alive. Then $200 was a small fortune.

Bernie made a little over $400 in commissions as a cigar salesman. Lily and Rose had been paying most of the rent. In Cleveland, in the late 30's, two hundred dollars got you a large four-bedroom apartment on the Park. Two bathrooms with an underground garage. Within walking distance of the art museum, Severance Hall, Rabbi Silver's

Temple and exclusive women's "shoppes." In such an apartment you were living well.

Aside from the rent, Lily and Rose bought all the clothes for his two little girls, bought most of the food because they loved to cook, and cluttered the bathroom with drying underwear and silk stockings. Not something he'd talk about with his poker buddies in the back of the Texaco. If he did cut himself loose from his sisters-in-law, he'd be leaping into space. Jumping off the Cuyahoga bridge. "Sink or swim, Bernie!" A small voice in his head said, "Don't be an idiot. You've got it made! Don't screw it up!" But he intended screwing it up.

Tonight he'd ANNOUNCE they'd have to go. Of course, many times before he had vowed the same thing. Each time when he came home, DETERMINED, his resolve would fail. He'd walk in at seven o'clock in the evening, see his wife, Peg, the sisters, Lily and Rose, and a fourth woman from the building, chatting around the card table with a hot game of mah-jongg going full blast. A haze of cigarette smoke shutting out the world. Laughter and squeals when one of them declared "*Kong*" or "*Maj.*" His two daughters, Sissie and Penny, sprawled on the floor dressing and undressing their dolls. This is a way to greet a man when he comes home?

Each time it was the same:

"Hello, Bernie," Peg called in her husky cigarette voice, "I think there's something still warm in the oven."

That was all he got. No one looked up or paid him any attention. An immigrant in alien country. He'd drop his overcoat on a hall chair and go into the kitchen for dinner. Eating alone, scanning the Cleveland Press sports section. An outsider in this universe of women. Any wonder that after such a welcome, Bernie would leave for an evening of poker at the back of the Texaco? Many times he didn't come home until ten, eleven or midnight, and wasn't missed. Poker was three nights a week in the back of the Texaco. Marty Katz, his bookie, orga-

MARK OF THE DREIDEL

nized it. Hot corned beef on rye was brought in so nobody had to leave hungry, even if they'd lost a bundle. These guys were his friends. "Come on in, Bernie. Here's a spot." Some were even on the team when he played second base for Glenville High.

Marty, the bookie, gave him a bear hug. "You feel lucky tonight, Bernie? You feel lucky?"

When he finally got home, Peg would say, "Hello, Bernie. Where you been?" then not wait for an answer but disappear into the bathroom to do her facial.

The sisters had to leave. Bernie would be master of his own home again! Easy to say. But how would he pay the rent on a cigar salesman's commissions?

"Who the hell cares! I'll manage somehow!" his inner voice bluffed. But a hundred-a-week commissions don't allow the lush lifestyle to which Bernie was accustomed, and to which Peg and his two little girls were accustomed. Would Peg side with her sisters, ask Bernie to leave? What about that? The tables turning? Would *he* go? Ah hah!

To tell you the truth, Bernie had it easy. Plenty of money coming in, considering what the sisters gave. He had no responsibility around the apartment. The women ran the place. His commissions were his to spend. He set aside half in Cleveland Trust savings, a habit learned from his father. The rest was to shmooze his customers. And to lose. If you had plenty to lose, people liked you. And at poker, horses, numbers, Bernie knew how to lose. It was nobody's business. He earned it. He could lose it. Peg didn't have to know.

His Peg was something else. In her time such a beauty! More than Bernie ever dreamed he could have. A figure. Wide hips. Legs that danced. A big enough bust. Lush curls of blond hair. Perfect long hands. Red nails. Elegant. That husky cigarette voice. Even the way Peg held it up to her face, turned and ready to draw. Class. He was totally

MARK OF THE DREIDEL

shocked when she said, "Yes." She said "Yes" to me? Bernie Kinsman? All he had going for him was playing second base for Glenville High. And he talked big. But then the sisters moved in to help with the rent. "Don't worry, Bernie, we're glad to contribute. Peg should live nice," Said Lily. "She's a special thing."

Growing up, Peg was the doll of her family. People wanted to be with her. She was no brain, but who cares? Rose and Lily had brains. What good did it do them?

"You both should live in a nice apartment," said Rose, "we're glad to help. There's plenty of room here. We won't be in the way. You'll see." He saw. In no time at all, he was the one in the way. Peg even produced daughters instead of sons to increase the odds.

Through the years, let me tell you, the gloss wore off. Beauty you get used to. You see that face and figure every day, naked and not naked. In makeup and plain. You get used to it. It becomes without value. Not that it has *no* value. It's just *without* value. Like furniture. Always been there. Always will be there. Why concern yourself?

This was the night to settle things. He threw open the door. The women were finishing up a maj-jongg game.

"Hello, Bernie," said Peg, "I think there's still some dinner in the oven."

"To hell with dinner! Lily and Rose, I think you'd better... another place to live." ...so choking with emotion, he couldn't get the words out.

"Your husband's drunk," said Rose.

"Take him into the bathroom and run cold water on his neck," said Lily, "that always worked with my husband." Lily had been married to a railroad man for three months. He died on a trip, twelve years ago. She lived on his pension. And he never came home drunk.

"Bernie," said Peg, "you'd better lie down."

MARK OF THE DREIDEL

"I said I want my home back! Tell your sisters to move out. Tomorrow, Peg. Tomorrow! In the morning!"

Sissie, his oldest, looked up from a book she was reading on the floor. "Mommy, what's wrong with Daddy?"

"Honey, you're talking like a fool," said Peg. "And don't shout. Sissie's doing her homework. You want her to fail second grade?"

"I really want them out tonight! Tomorrow, the latest, or I'll start throwing their things in the hall! You'd like that better?"

"Bernie, if you're upset about some customer, we'll talk privately," said Peg. "Let us girls finish this game first. Go into the kitchen and eat. Should I make you some fresh coffee?"

Of course, it was embarrassing. For everybody. Most of all for Bernie. The women didn't take him seriously. He stormed out of the apartment for a walk in the park. A hot summer evening. What was he doing? He knew he could never afford this place on his own. For godsakes, he lived in a better neighborhood than his customers.

He walked. The lights of businesses were still flourishing. The City Ice and Fuel sign still hadn't been fixed. It stood forty feet in the air on a iron scaffold. Flashing in red neon. It used to say "Hot Enough?" But someone threw a stone or maybe the circuit went bad. It flashed "Enough" now. Bernie could understand that. He lit up a panatela. Private stock, one of the samples he was supposed to hand out to buyers. What the hell, a few for his pocket wouldn't be missed. Goes with the job. For eight years, Bernie had worked for J. Klein, Wholesale Tobacco and Sundries, building up a great territory in East Cleveland, Collingwood and around the Jewish neighborhood of 105th Street. When he started the territory, J. Klein was nothing. Schuman & Sons Tobacco Merchants dominated the trade. Bernie was streetwise enough to know that buyers don't stock cigars because of aroma. Tickets to major fights, baseball games, twenty dollars in an envelope to the store manager, a bottle of Seagrams; that sold tobacco. Shaving a few cents off a gross of cigars was Joe Klein's idea of merchandising. "I'm working for a complete idiot," thought Bernie.

White Owls, Garcia Operas, Havana Select. What names cigars had. Like racehorses or custom-built cars. Suprema Pentalla! Names with weight. Names with aroma. "All the same schlock," Bernie would say. "Cigars don't sell cigars. Taking care of people sells cigars." Nobody wants a good five-cent cigar. They want a fifty-cent cigar for twenty cents. Even if it's only worth five cents. Joe Klein never got that message. He thought selling cigars was simply filling empty spaces on a shelf. He never got the message, but he owned the business.

"Someday, when I go on my own —-" no, that wasn't Bernie. He wasn't a fighter.

Three weeks later, Bernie held the door open. There was a tearful farewell in the apartment. "I'll never forgive you for this," sobbed a red-faced Lily. She was lugging two suitcases. While holding the door, a smug Bernie smoked the biggest, most awful-smelling cigar J. Klein stocked.

Sissie was crying, too. "Can we come visit you, Aunt Lily?"

"Come, come," said Rose, because Lily was too moved to talk. "Come and stay even."

"Can I come, too?" asked Penny, the five-year-old.

Lily was overcome. She dropped her luggage, knelt down and opened her arms. "Oh, darlings, come to me. Give your Aunt Lily a big hug."

Peg looked at Bernie, with a LOOK. "*She what you've done. Giving such pain to our little girls. And for what?*" Because even now, no one knew why Bernie was upset. They thought things were fine.

The apartment was like a cavern without Lily and Rose. The little girls didn't know their father, except as the man who came home late and ate in the kitchen. Peg and Bernie lived a divided marriage. She

MARK OF THE DREIDEL

with home. He with work and poker. They were strangers now stranded on an island. For a while Peg shopped to keep herself busy. New clothes for her and the girls. Bernie would come home and see boxes scattered around the living room. Halle's and Lindners and Goldweir Shoppes. Each box the commission of a big order.

His was the only paycheck. He tried loading his customers with more cigars. But rapidly all the open spaces were filled. Joe Klein's business philosophy of keeping shelves full came to pass. There was no Rose and Lily to fall back on. He still had savings at Cleveland Trust to draw. But wouldn't you know—Bernie got lucky. Two longshot horses on two different days decided to run for a living. His pockets were full.

Then it hit him.

He woke one morning in a sweat. There was an awful pain in his side. He took four aspirin and lay back down. "What's the matter, Bernie?" Peg brought him in his coffee.

"I don't know," said Bernie, "I got this pain. I don't think I'm going to call on anybody today."

"That's all right, honey. You just lay there and I'll take care of you. Should I call Mr. Klein and tell him you're sick?"

"Don't worry. It's none of his business. My customers will wait." He knew they were loyal to him. Al Litcomb, cigar buyer for the chain of Merchant Tobacco Stores, was like a brother. Bernie had gotten him six tickets for the Louis-Braddock fight. Litcomb was in seventh heaven. Loyal? Bernie could depend on his customers. No question!

Pain came and went. On the bed, on the sofa, he tried to find a comfortable position. Peg massaged his back. "What can I do for you? Tell me, Bernie. I hate to see you suffer so."

That night was something else. Pain he couldn't believe. A mole chewing away at his insides. Pain moved from this side to that. More aspirin. No effect. He tried laying in a hot bath. Pain wouldn't go away.

MARK OF THE DREIDEL

This must be kidney stones. He'd heard guys talk about having them. They'd made jokes. What a joke! Up. Down. Even flat on the floor, trying to find a way to ease the ache. At two in the morning, he tried walking it off outside. The brisk night air was a change from the hot apartment. Yes, it felt better to walk. He walked in the park, and then toward Mt. Sinai Hospital, the only building showing lights at this time of night.

The City Ice and Fuel sign flashed *Enough*. "Ain't it the truth," thought Bernie, "I got enough of this pain!" Sweat went up his back and collected on his forehead, like condensation from a steam kettle that had been boiling all night. In the apartment, it was quiet when Bernie came back. The pain had eased a bit. The walk did him good. He got into bed.

"Feeling better, honey," Peg said in a drowsy mumble, "you want I should rub your back again?" Getting no response, she relaxed into sleep.

For no reason, at nine in the morning it ended. The pain stopped. Bernie must have sweated five gallons. The sheets had to be hung to dry. Two days without rest. He was exhausted. He told Peg to call Joe Klein. Tell him Bernie was going to take a few days off. She came back with the news. "Mr Klein said take all the time you need. He's giving your territory to his new son-in-law."

"That's MY territory," yelled Bernie, "he can't give away MY territory. My customers won't stand for it." Don't bet on it.

By the end of the week, Bernie felt rested. His first impulse was to confront Joe Klein. But what could he say? There was nothing in writing. He assured Peg things would get better. He had lots of friends. It would be a bitter pill, but he might approach Schuman & Sons, his old competitor.

At dinner Peg said, "Maybe I could get a job."

MARK OF THE DREIDEL

"You're a nice kid to offer, Peg, but what could you do?" said Bernie with a smirk.

"Don't say that!" She kicked his leg under the table. "People always said that about me. I'm not dumb, you know."

In a week, Peg had a job at Modern Dry Cleaning, working the counter because she was attractive. As weeks went by, she learned to unload the big machines when the back room got shorthanded. Her boss liked her. Peg, working from 7:30 in the morning to 5:00 at night, was gone before the girls got up for school. Bernie had to fix their bag lunches. He was terrible making lunches. Sissie decided to teach him how. "Watch me, Dad. First, you smear on the mayo...." In no time she had her father trained.

"What a smart kid I have," thought Bernie.

He was home in the afternoon when they returned from school. At first they had nothing to say to each other. The girls were still mad at losing the Aunts and extra gifts they got two or three times a week. But one afternoon, out of boredom, they taught Bernie mah-jongg and he taught them poker. Penny could figure the odds on drawing a straight, a full house or three of a kind. She was a natural. Once she bluffed her dad into folding because he thought she had aces. She had nothing. *Bubkes!* Even he couldn't bluff that good. "My Penny! A chip off the old block!"

A few days later he brought up a pile of empty cedar cigar boxes from the basement storeroom. On the dining room table that afternoon, the girls made doll houses with Bernie's help. When Peg got home from work that night, the first thing she said was "Bernie, you shouldn't leave such a mess on the table." She went to lie down. "I've been on my feet all day."

Bernie tried selling shoes and housewares door to door, but nothing suited his personality. He swallowed his pride and talked with old Curt Schuman, his former competitor in the cigar business. Schuman gave

MARK OF THE DREIDEL

him a small territory in Cleveland Heights, plus a piece that included many of his old customers from J. Klein. He'd be selling head to head against Joe Klein's son-in-law. Revenge would be sweet. It wasn't. For instance, Al Litcomb said Klein was knocking a dollar off every two dozen White Owls. When Bernie called Schuman about that, he was told they weren't in business to give away profit. "Order takers give away profit. Salesmen sell!" Bernie was in no mood for a lecture but he kept his mouth shut.

Bernie said he'd match Klein's deal out of his own commission. Litcomb said it would now take a dollar and a half to get the order. Bernie had to write up something or he'd lose the territory. Who'd have thought his friend, Litcomb, would squeeze him that way? Times had changed. He couldn't reach into his pockets to buy fight tickets or whiskey to impress customers. The nest egg at Cleveland Trust Bank he wouldn't touch. He needed operating capital but Schuman wouldn't give him an advance.

Maybe he could borrow from Marty Katz. Over the years Marty made a good income from him. Marty was happy to help. Eight hundred for six months at ten percent interest per month. That much! What about old time's sake? "I'm already giving you a deal," said Marty, putting his arm around Bernie's shoulder. "The others are paying fourteen and fifteen percent, so you're practically stealing the money."

Bernie said he'd think about it

"Anytime, I'm here for you. By the way, you're making yourself scarce from poker. Game next Saturday night. You might be lucky."

"I'll see," said Bernie, "I'll see." When you're up against the wall, where are your friends?

That day there was an accident at Modern Dry Cleaners. A rusted pipe to the cleaning chemical tank ruptured. Cleaning fluid was three inches deep. The fumes knocked Peg out. They took her to Mt. Sinai.

MARK OF THE DREIDEL

Bernie got a call when he got home. "Mrs. Kinsman has been brought in for observation. A precaution." Out of the blue, such a call! He left a message for the girls and went right to Mt. Sinai. Peg was okay, but they wanted to keep her overnight.

Somehow Lily and Rose found out. They called Bernie and began yelling at him on the phone. *It was his fault. They never should have left.* He slammed the phone down. The next morning when he went to the hospital to take Peg home, the Aunts were there. There was hugging and crying and dirty looks.

"What has he done to you!"

Peg calmed them down. It was an accident.

"What kind of man are you," yelled Rose in Bernie's face, "forcing our sister to work with deadly chemicals. Electrocution is too good for you!" Bernie couldn't answer.

Lily and Rose wanted to take Peg to Florida. "I mean who needs this winter?" They were going on vacation. Peg could get her health back. No, she was alright. But thanks. Peg knew Bernie needed her income.

Modern cleaners was closed until they could get the building cleaned and aired out. The County Health Department put a seal on the door. Peg was out of a job.

In a week it would be Hanukkah. "You want to do something for your daughters?" said Peg. "Take them to the dreidel party at the temple." On Saturday night, the night of his poker game. For some reason he felt lucky. On the other hand...*choose, Bernie Kinsman.*

Bernie had seldom set foot in a temple since his bar mitzvah. He was not what you'd call a good Jew, by any stretch. For Peg to get him to High Holy Days was like pulling a cat into the bathtub.

"Bernie, give the girls a dollar for a dreidel. They'll need it for the party."

MARK OF THE DREIDEL

Bernie refused. He turned red. "A dreidel! That's Jewish gambling!" You'd never believe the kind of things he was saying, just to get out of it. "What kind of hypocrites are running that place to offer gambling to children!"

"You bet on the horses, Bernie," Peg said.

"How do you know?" his face flushed with guilt.

"Never mind. I know. I'm no dummy."

"So do I win? No. Shouldn't my children learn from my mistakes!"

"It's only a toy, Bernie. It's not going to drive them into a life of crime for godsakes."

"Never a dreidel in my house. Never." He wouldn't take them, so Peg did.

Left home alone that Saturday night, he pondered going to the poker game. What if Peg found out? And he was still angry at Marty Katz for trying to bleed him. He stayed home.

In late April, Peg was tired a lot. She couldn't work a whole day. Lots of foods started to disagree with her. She smoked two packs a day. Sissie noticed something. On the side of Peg's face, a small red sore. "It looks like a dreidel on your face, Mommy," said Sissie.

Then Penny chimed in. "Daddy wouldn't let us have a dreidel in the house and now Mommy's got one on her cheek!" She felt awful. Dizzy. Pain in her back. She was becoming less of a blond and didn't care. The doctor couldn't explain it. He put her in Mt. Sinai, only a long walk from the apartment. "Observation." A day or two grew into a week. Peg got a call from her sisters in Florida. Yes, she was feeling better. A lie.

Bernie spent a lot of time with Peg at the hospital. Back and forth from his sales calls, at least five or six hours a day. Until late in the evening.

Children weren't allowed to visit. One evening Bernie took Sissie and Penny outside on the hospital lawn. They sat on the grass, under Peg's third floor window. The children could see that small figure, way up there, and were told to believe it was their mother. They didn't believe it. As Bernie leaned out the window with Peg, to wave at his children below, he could see in the distance the Ice and Fuel sign, *Enough*.

By her bedside, Bernie would hold Peg's hand. Those long elegant fingers. She hadn't done her nails, which made her feel dowdy. And her hair wasn't perfect soft waves anymore. Bernie talked about things on his mind. One night he said, "You know what surprised me, Peg?"

"No, what?"

"**When I asked** your sisters to leave, you knew that would put us in **tough financial** shape. But you let them go. You didn't throw me out instead."

"That surprised you?" she asked, incredulous.

"Yeh. I thought I might be gone."

"But Bernie, you're my husband," Peg said. "I made you a promise."

The doctors gave her this test and that test, but found nothing. They told Bernie to take her home and let her rest a lot.

"What's wrong with me?" she asked over and over as she lay in bed.

Bernie's younger sister, Sarah, came to cook and clean, because he was not able to get dinner for Peg and his daughters. But he did put them to sleep. He told the girls stories of spending summers on his uncle's farm. What he did as a kid. How he'd wander whole days at Euclid Beach. What was that? An amusement park on Lake Erie. "When Mom gets well, we'll all go."

She did get better. It was late in May. Flowers were out and Peg wanted to see them. She sat outside in the sunshine. He told Peg that he'd promised the girls we'd all go to Euclid Beach when she got better. Peg's eyes lighted up. She hadn't been there since she was a kid.

By mid-June, she was a lot better. They drove to Euclid Beach. What a day they had. The girls had never been on a roller coaster. Sissie was

MARK OF THE DREIDEL

frightened, but little Penny wanted to go again and again. The Dodgem…little electric cars bumping into each other…they couldn't get enough. A kind of fun they'd never before enjoyed as a family. At dusk, they walked along the sandy beach of Lake Erie and the girls threw stones into the waves.

Nice as that was, they shouldn't have done it. Peg caught a chill when they walked on the lake shore. In three days, she was back in bed. Her long hands were shaking. The mark of the dreidel on her cheek was now the size of a nickel. It had thickness to it, and it hurt. She was losing weight and was no longer a natural blonde. The doctors put her back in Mt. Sinai. Bernie couldn't do anything to help her. She was slipping away.

He called Lily and Rose, who were by now back from Florida. It hurt, but he asked them to take the girls so he could spend more time with Peg. The doctors watched her for a few days and then they pulled him aside. "Mr. Kinsman, there are a lot of things we don't know. Your wife's condition is, maybe, cancer. We need to do an exploratory operation to help us find out." They'd have to decide no later than tomorrow.

Bernie went home to say goodbye to his girls. Lily and Rose were taking them this afternoon. Bernie's sister, Sarah, had made dinner. The Aunts hadn't arrived yet. Bernie tried to explain to his daughters about their mother. It was terrible for him. He took the two girls in his arms, tears began to run.

"Will Mommy get better?" asked Penny. He couldn't answer because the small sobs in his throat smeared the words.

In the hospital, Peg's pillow was wet. She pulled him to her. "Don't let them cut me up, Bernie. I don't have a scar on me anywhere. Don't let them cut me up. I'll get better. I promise." Bernie stroked her hands. This was to be the painful end of everything in his life.

MARK OF THE DREIDEL

He stayed with her, remembering how she stayed with him the night he fought the kidney stones. Peg was mumbling. She turned this way and that. Her eyes did not see. Did she know him?

At two in the morning he left her sleeping fitfully to go for a walk. He had to clear his thoughts. Tomorrow the doctors expected an answer. Bernie walked outside, around the hospital grounds. The streets were darkened. Lonely. Across the park the Art Museum was lit up. The red neon sign flashed in the distance, *Enough*. Harsh lights flooded the driveway at the emergency entrance of the hospital. Then out of the dark, Bernie saw a figure walking toward him. The man seemed to be wearing a heavy overcoat, even though this was a summer evening. He came closer. They were about to pass on the walkway. Bernie looked into the man's eyes. The head was hooded. He couldn't see a face. Only the eyes. Only eyes. Bernie felt a gentleness wash over him. This would be all right. "I can't explain it," he said later. Was this a Messenger of Death? Did it say he'd lost Peg? Had she died peacefully? Was this the messenger of *Enough*?

Bernie went back up to Peg's room. He wanted to hurry, yes, but then he didn't want to know. At the door he looked at her in the dim light. No movement. Her delicate hands rested at her side. Dead? He was afraid to approach her. Had the shadow figure wiped away her life? He went to her side. She was hardly moving. Rest. He knelt and held her hand. It was warm. He got up to look out the window. Was there a figure walking down there? Nothing. Then an ambulance drove away from the emergency entrance. And over in the distance, the City Ice and Fuel sign flashed.

In three days she was sitting up. In a week she was back home, able to get out of bed and walk around the apartment. She started making dinner. Amazing. And she was so sick! With what? The incurable word. But it couldn't have been that. Here she was getting well. Some pious people to whom I've told this story say they can't believe it. Why would God perform a miracle for a schmuck like Bernie? A practicing Jew?

MARK OF THE DREIDEL

Are you kidding? Did he give to the poor? Are you kidding? He wasted his money playing poker in the back of the Texaco, eating fat corned beef on rye. Aren't there Jews more deserving of a miracle? Thus said the pious. And they were probably right. Except they don't run the universe. Do they know what's in God's eyes?

Bernie failed a lot. He gambled but couldn't win. He sold cigars but couldn't keep his territory. He ignored his lovely Peg, but wept at losing her. He paid little attention to his daughters, till months before the end. He was late to realize life. He didn't even, when things got rough, turn to God. If we believe this story, God turned to him.

So? What's new? It proves that God will wait longer than you can hold out. God does not live by thunderbolts alone. God is also patient. Things got better. Bernie's territory started to pay off. The son-in-law, such a know-it-all who was going to inherit the business, was an idiot. Besides, he never gave out free cigars to his customers. Too cheap. The girls missed their father. Although they loved staying with the present-giving Aunts, they wanted to come home.

Peg didn't go back to work. Modern Dry Cleaners had insurance. Because she had been in the hospital three times, they worried about a long-term medical bill, or a lawsuit over her death. You could trace nothing to the spill, but who knows what a jury would decide? Without asking or quibbling, Prudential offered a one-time settlement. It was, for those days, ENOUGH.

At the end of the summer, they all went again to Euclid Beach. Sissie tried the roller coaster, Penny went three times. They walked again on the beach at dusk. But Peg dressed warm.

In six months, Bernie Kinsman was dead. A heart attack. Suddenly. Who could predict?

He did smoke strong cigars. And the word "exercise" he didn't know. Unless shuffling a poker deck was an Olympic sport.

MARK OF THE DREIDEL

A few months! Everything was going so right. What a time to take him away! Does this make sense to you? Me neither. A little happiness was beginning to creep into his life. He was becoming friends with Peg and the two girls…then poof! It's all over.

The red neon sign blinked, "*Enough,*" "*Enough.*"

Less than a year, from a whole lifetime.

You've learned something from this?

Think about it. Don't be a fool.

What else can I say?

THE DREIDEL MAKER AND THE RICH MAN

In Cleveland, Ohio before the modern times of which we are a part, there was a small Orthodox Jewish community centered around the shul, Congregation B'nai Mosheh, on East 105th Street. Many Jewish families lived nearby, close enough to walk to the synagogue on *Shabbos*. The orthodox custom was that one shouldn't ride in a car, even a streetcar or a bus, on the Sabbath. One shouldn't force another to work on the day of rest. It was a close-knit community. Within seven blocks were two kosher butcher shops. In those days you could buy a live chicken from a cage, have it killed by a *shohet*, a ritual slaughterer trained to kill in a humane manner, have the chicken plucked, dressed and wrapped in white wax paper and handed to you while you waited. Guaranteed fresh! And bakeries…what bakeries! At Kindlesman's or Sand's you could buy chocolate cake bars, smothered in coconut. What

THE DREIDEL MAKER AND THE RICH MAN

deliciousness! Everything was baked TODAY. That was before cellophane wrapping decreed that nothing should have taste anymore. Fresh bagels. Not like now, frozen. You would think they are selling them to Eskimos. How could people choose a frozen bagel…on purpose?

Within a few blocks were shoe stores owned by members of the congregation, a travel agency to send money back to relatives in the old country, a branch of the Cleveland Trust bank. Even a dreidel maker, Reuben.

Reuben Abraham was a carver of wood. He had a red face and bushy white hair above a big nose. Picture an excited polar bear. I say "picture" even though I've never seen one in person. A carver of wood. Of course, in a Jewish community, especially orthodox, you can't make a living carving graven images. The market doesn't exist. You carve what people will buy. What is that? A pair of candlesticks from lemon wood or cedar. A fancy oak mezuzah for the doorway. And dreidels. It was from dreidels that Reuben became a little famous, as famous as you can become within twenty miles from home. He was famous for something else, which I'll tell you about in a minute.

The dreidels that Reuben carved had a body that curved inward, just in the softest way. So as they spun, each would sing an angelic tone. As if there were a "being" inside which came to life as the dreidel turned. A magical thing to hear. Charming as Reuben's dreidels were, they were still a children's toy. So how much could they be worth? Am I right? He never got rich from carving dreidels. Also, if you ask me, he spent too much time finishing each one just so. How much can you charge? So he never got rich. In a word, he was a poor carver. Not a poor carver. But just poor.

He lived in two small rooms behind his shop on Pierpont Avenue. Old patched clothes he wore. The knives he carved with were by now thin slivers of steel from being sharpened over and over. After all, could

THE DREIDEL MAKER AND THE RICH MAN

a poor carver afford new knives each year? Of course not. You make do with what you have.

Before I said he was famous for something else. This is it. Poor as he was, he never turned a beggar away empty-handed. A person in financial trouble could always count on Reuben for help. You say, "So? That's how it should be according to Jewish law." Of course, you are right. But how many live that way? Reuben did. However little he had and anyone could see he had little, he was always willing to share it with someone worse off. *Tzedakah.* Charity. Good deeds. Reuben, the dreidel maker, had laid up a storehouse in Heaven.

In this small community of Congregation B'nai Mosheh, he was both respected and loved. Rabbi Selzer always made a special effort to shake Reuben's hand after Services. If a stranger came to visit from Toledo or New York, people would take them to Reuben's workshop on Pierpont Avenue and point it out.

"A great Talmudic scholar he is not," they would say. "But he has charity in his heart. Even more blessed."

He was respected. Do you follow me? Some even whispered that he was one of the thirty-six saints upon whom God depends to save the world. As for Reuben, he never made a big deal out of it. Self important he was not. He never served on any committee at the shul. He never dressed fancy. He lived simply, as a carver of wood.

Let me give you an example. It was a cold November night. Raining. There was a knock on Reuben's door. He was working late. This was his busy season. When else in the year do people need dreidels except at Hanukkah time? You carve when you've got customers. He opened the door. Who should be standing there, shivering? Morry Pelsky, the butcher's helper. It seems his wife needed a gallbladder operation badly. And he had just spent all his savings and more to bring his mother over from the old country, Hungary. There were the tickets to

THE DREIDEL MAKER AND THE RICH MAN

buy. Lawyers to arrange things. Officials to bribe. You know how it is. Or maybe you don't.

That was the time the flood of Jews from Europe was still pouring. Anyone who could was fleeing Hitler and Poland and the hatred mixed with the mother's milk in all those countries. Tears cloud my eyes when I am alone sometimes. How can we call ourselves humankind, when we so willingly drive each other around like cattle? How is it we can still look in mirrors? Ah, but that's another story.

Reuben laid his carving tools down and put his arm around Pelsky's wet shoulder. "How much do you need for the operation?" he asked.

"The doctor said between eighty and a hundred thirty dollars," replied Pelsky, turning his cap round and round between his fingers. That much money! In those days it was probably six weeks' wages for a butcher's helper.

"Come tomorrow night," said Reuben. "We'll see." He patted Morry on the shoulder and he let him out.

The next night, when Pelsky returned, Reuben gave him a hundred fifty dollars wrapped in a torn piece of newspaper. Pelsky thanked him and thanked him and thanked him. But Reuben said nothing. He just nodded slowly.

Though Reuben was poor, those were tough times, not so easy like today. Some members of the congregation were rich. Wealthy men who had made their mark on America. Men with two shoe stores, or an apartment building here and there. Of these, the richest man in the shul was a guy named Norman Gold, formerly Goldfarber. He owned a house with two bathrooms, plus a place to powder. Each of his three children had a bedroom of their own. Goldfarber, excuse me, Gold, stood over six feet tall. He had deep eyes, surrounded by shadows. He wore glasses without rims. He was well set. He was also tight as a rusted bolt. From Gold, if you got a nickel you gave a dollar's worth of sweat.

THE DREIDEL MAKER AND THE RICH MAN

He was known throughout the community as a miser. A man this rich doesn't have to be a cheapskate, right?

For instance, a poor man came to Gold's door on the second night of Hanukkah. It was snowing.

"Excuse me, Mr. Gold. Could you lend me a few dollars so I could buy Hanukkah presents for my children?"

Gold did not reply. He simply stood in the open doorway. His silence forced the poor man to continue to beg.

"I worked for Meyer's Furniture, fixing damaged chairs. But now he has gone out of business. I have looked for two months."

Gold interrupted. "You from around here?"

The man nodded.

"Then you are a liar," said Gold. "Everyone in this community knows I don't waste money on charity. You'll have to beg somewhere else." He shut the door in the poor man's face.

Now to those who knew Gold, such behavior was no surprise. It was to be expected from Miser Gold, the rich man.

Anyway, as God wills it, one day Norman Gold died. His widow wept. Rabbi Selzer quickly called together a meeting of the board of the shul and the burial committee. What were they going to do about Norman Gold?

Let me explain. Many years ago when this congregation was young, they purchased a piece of land out on Eddy Road for a cemetery. Back then it was rolling hills and trees. Not built up like it is today. This cemetery was a very holy place to the shul. Members got together and put up a handsome stone and brick wall all around it.

It was a holy place, but the holiest part was along the eastern wall. Because theoretically it was closest to the city of Jerusalem. Of course, plots there were the most expensive, too. Now if the eastern wall was

THE DREIDEL MAKER AND THE RICH MAN

the most holy, conversely along the western wall was where they buried the very poor. Paupers. The unknowns. The people with nothing. Over the years, parts of the western wall had broken down. Huge chunks of brick and stone lay on the ground. A wire fence had been strung up to fill the open spaces. It didn't look so hot. And about nine or ten years ago the people who owned the property next to the western wall decided to put up a factory. A factory! Next to an Orthodox Jewish cemetery! The board of the shul appealed to the Highest Authorities. But the Highest Authorities didn't pay any attention. The factory made batteries for cars and trucks.

It was decided to bury Norman Gold along the western fence, where the wall had broken down. Such a thing was unheard of. To bury the richest man in the Congregation next to a battery factory! Gold's widow wailed and protested. But Rabbi Selzer turned a deaf ear. "He should be grateful we're burying him even at the west wall. That…that miser!"…the Rabbi was reported to have shouted.

The day of the funeral, the board of the shul didn't even bother to follow the hearse to the cemetery. At the graveside were only Rabbi Selzer, Gold's widow and children and a few relatives. Thus the life of a miser was closed.

A few weeks passed. A young woman, Mrs. Klein, lost her husband in a milk wagon accident. She had two small children and no relatives in Cleveland. Someone told her to see Reuben. He wouldn't turn her away empty-handed. When she knocked on the door of his shop on Pierpont Avenue, he let her in. Reuben listened to her story. Then he shook his head and said "I'm sorry.…But wait." And he went to the two rooms behnd his workshop and came back with a half loaf of rye bread and a tin can full of coins. It was not quite four dollars. These he poured into her hand. A half loaf of bread and a few coins! Not the help she expected. Mrs. Klein was brokenhearted…for she had been led to believe…you understand.

THE DREIDEL MAKER AND THE RICH MAN

Then a few days later another person came to Reuben for help. He, too, was turned away. "What is this? What is happening in our community?" people asked. The board of the shul voted to send Rabbi Selzer as a delegation to visit Reuben. The Rabbi should ask why he had suddenly turned against the poor.

"Come in, Rabbi," said Reuben. "Will you share with me a cup of tea?"

The Rabbi sat in a mended wicker chair. They talked of this and that. Finally the Rabbi asked, "How is it, Reuben my son, that you have suddenly turned your eyes against the needy among us?"

"I am a poor man myself, Rabbi."

"I see that. But even so, over the years you've been so generous." The Rabbi was perplexed.

"Let me tell you a story, Rabbi," Reuben began, "Many years ago a rich man came to me I should carve some candlesticks. A gift for his mother. We struck up a friendship. He gave me a large amount of money to help people I found in need. From time to time he would bring me more. Whatever I asked for he gave without question. On one condition."

"The condition was I never reveal his name. As luck would have it, some weeks ago the man died. Before there was always money to help. Now I have nothing more to give. You see for yourself, Rabbi, I am a poor man."

Rabbi Selzer was both shocked and ashamed. To give without you yourself being known, that is one of the highest forms of Jewish charity.

The Rabbi called together the board of the shul. Even though it was late on Thursday afternoon and raining, they all walked together to the cemetery on Eddy Road, to visit the fresh grave of Miser Gold. Rabbi Selzer threw himself down on the soft earth. He wept as he begged forgiveness from the soul of Miser Gold.

THE DREIDEL MAKER AND THE RICH MAN

"Forgive me!" he sobbed. "Forgive me for JUDGING. FORGIVE ME FOR JUDGING YOU."

In his will, Rabbi Selzer asked to be buried with the poor, next to the western wall, alongside the grave of Miser Gold.

And so he was.

SOUR MARRIAGE, SWEET DREIDEL

It was not the best of marriages, except maybe by your standards. Two years now, Sissie and Babe were one, living as two. He was 29, she was 32. Ah hah, you say, that's the problem. To which I reply, Ah hah, you don't know what you're talking about.

He said she was a terrible housekeeper.

She said he spent too much time playing baseball. Unless you've just got *kishkes* for brains, you know those weren't real reasons. It's just what they argued about.

For instance, he would come home after a game with a few fellas, not only Jewish boys either. They'd bring something to drink, some potato salad and corned beef sandwiches from Levy's. Sissie would hide herself in the bedroom, reading a book. Or she wouldn't be in the apartment at all. She'd be visiting her parents, Flo and Maishe Mandelbaum.

SOUR MARRIAGE, SWEET DREIDEL

"If he has a right to go out at night and play the second base, I have a right to visit my dear parents. After all, Cleveland Heights is still in America, which is a free country the last I heard." To tell the truth, they were not her "dear" parents. But a little stretching is expected in every argument.

Here was a marriage you wouldn't want to place bets on, unless they gave you odds like maybe six months. They met at a temple function, a wedding reception for Sissie's nineteen-year-old cousin! Sissie was roiling with envy. "This snip is already married at nineteen," she thought. "I am almost thirty and still single. I am not even SEEING anybody." Her younger sister, Rebecca, was already married, very well, to Robert Lindsey Greene, Attorney-at-Law. Sissie still lived at home, taking sides in her parents' arguments.

"Why not me getting married?" she agonized. "I have brains. I dress well. I am clever." But real life is more complicated than that. This one she didn't like. And that one didn't like her. Of the few eligible Jewish men her age, there weren't a bundle of choices. Even so, she was "the critic". Some were stupid, or dressed like 'Litvaks' or didn't catch her humor. A million reasons she had. And for those flaws she failed to notice, her father was only too happy to point them out.

Fine and dandy. But she was the one who was 29! Easy for him to talk. His life was already lived. She would soon be 30 and going nowhere. Her younger sister, Rebecca, whom she considered a brainless nit, had nonetheless hooked a fresh fish like Robert Lindsey Greene, attorney. "Why not me?" she thought. "I have charm and I certainly have enough brains for an attorney. So why haven't I hooked a similar prize?"

What she didn't know, because her father, Maishe Mandelbuam, never told her, was that she had no charm. None at all. She was critical of everyone, except her father and herself, of course. No one was good enough for her. "You want me to go out with Harold Wiener!" she

SOUR MARRIAGE, SWEET DREIDEL

scoffed at her mother. "He's still got pimples from junior high." And when her mother suggested Alex Saperstein, another nice boy, she condescended to explain, "Mother! Alex Saperstein is not my idea of a date. He works in a hardware store with his father. A HARDware store, Mother! He never gets his hands clean."

What could Flo Mandelbaum say? In any family argument Maishe always sided with Sissie against his wife. He never contradicted Sissie's judgment, because she'd learned over time to mouth exactly what her father would have said, a sure fire way to get approval. So what chance did Flo Mandelbaum have?

Maishe would monopolize dinner conversation, repeating a speech too loudly for the few listeners in the room. "Sissie's our eldest, Florence." He used his wife's full name when he was particularly irritated with her. "Are we supposed to force her out of her own home just to satisfy a few yentas who can't stand a girl not being married? Is it their business?"

But when 29 hit her, Sissie realized that being tied to Alex Saperstein was better than being an old maid. Besides, Alex now owned three hardware stores and numerous other business ventures. His fingernails were clean. Too late. He was tied to someone else.

At the wedding reception, she looked around, sizing up the men. There were no unattached attorneys. Without consulting her father, she decided to strike up a conversation with Babe Braverman. Babe was a pleasant enough man. No great brain. Still lived with his mother. A possible, even though he was involved with the City League baseball. Babe owned a produce truck that delivered house-to-house in various neighborhoods. A business and his alone. Given time, who knows?

Babe was at the buffet table, standing next to his mother. Sissie took a deep breath and went over to him.

"Hello, Mrs. Braverman. You're looking well."

SOUR MARRIAGE, SWEET DREIDEL

"Thank God I still have my health. Excuse me, my eyesight ain't so good anymore. You're one of the Mandelbaum girls?" Mrs. Braverman asked.

"Yes, Sissie."

"The older one. You know my son?"

"I don't know if we've ever met," said Sissie with painful coyness.

"This is my Babe. Babe, this is Sissie Mandelbaum. Her father is in the movie business."

"How do you do," Sissie offered her hand. "He only runs a small theater in Painsville, Mrs. Braverman."

"Anyway," she replied with a twinkle, "he's closer to William Powell than I am."

It was amazing, Mrs. Braverman thought to herself, that only yesterday she and Babe were arguing that he should find a nice Jewish girl. And who walks in?

"Excuse me, darling," said Mrs. Braverman, "my sister, Mollie, is motioning me over," And she left.

Sissie looked at Babe, and he looked at his departing mother. The pause was deafening. Who would say the next word?

"Nice wedding, wasn't it?" said Sissie.

"Sissie?" He pondered for a moment. "Yeh, I know your sister. Is she here?"

"No, she's vacationing in New York with her husband." Everyone knows my sister, thought Sissie.

"She's married? Boy, she was some beauty! Didn't she win a beauty contest or something?"

"Yes, it was here at the temple. She was Queen Esther for Purim three years in a row."

SOUR MARRIAGE, SWEET DREIDEL

"Oh yah, I remember now. Time sure flies, doesn't it." He waited for another long breath of silence to pass by. "Have you ever been out to one of my games?"

"What an absolutely dumb question," she thought. "Do I look like his sports fans? How could he be so dense?" "What kind of games do you play?" she asked sweetly.

"Baseball. Second base. Triple A City League. I'm on the Carnegie Auto Body Rockets. We've been in first place all year." He knew nothing else to say that could possibly be of interest.

"I heard the bride's dress cost over seven hundred dollars," she replied.

"Man, that's a lot! Can I get you some punch?" She shook her head no. "Would you like to come out and see a game? We're playing White Motors tomorrow night for the Division," he said.

"Where is it?" She couldn't believe this. Was she being talked into seeing a baseball game? She was and she went.

You ask, why did he bother with her and she with him? There was always pressure on a Jewish girl in this circle…Cleveland Heights, University Heights and Shaker Heights…to be married. As for Babe, to be totally truthful, while he was talking to Sissie he was imagining Rebecca. Who could blame him?

Babe's mother had been on him for years to find a nice girl. Stop playing around with the shiksas making eyes at you in the ballpark. "Bring me home at least once a nice Jewish girl! I'll make a wonderful pot roast for you."

His full name was Morton Felix Braverman, the youngest son in a family of six boys. Babe was everyone's favorite. He was a skinny, raw-boned young man, with a hawklike nose gentiles always associated with Jewish athletes. His older brothers went on to become dentists, lawyers and one even a fiddler for the Cleveland Symphony. Since Babe

SOUR MARRIAGE, SWEET DREIDEL

was the "baby" he was allowed to do whatever he wanted. What he wanted was to play second base on the Carnegie Auto Body Rockets, a famous City League team. He had been their star infielder since joining the team right out of Glenville High School in 1937.

Babe was a consistent 400-plus hitter and a scrappy infielder. The one Jewish boy on a team of Polacks, Germans and Irish. He was a great crowd pleaser. Nobody could understand where he got the power to hit so many home runs. But hit them he did, saving many a championship game in the ninth. For any Jewish boy growing up in Cleveland who loved baseball and whose mother wanted him to become a doctor, Babe was a nice hero to have around. Of course, second base isn't a living—not in the City League.

At 22, Babe took over his father's produce business, a flatbed Willys-Essex truck from which he sold fresh fruit and vegetables house-to-house on a regular route in East Cleveland and Cleveland Heights. In other words, a produce peddler. Was it a living? Didn't his father raise a family of six, all but one who went to college? Didn't he retire to a large apartment, owning the building of eight units? Starting with nothing in 1904 from Hungary, wouldn't you call that a living?

Sissie was a girl who never did anything around the house except side with her father against her mother. She was her father's pet. When Maishe would go to Chicago or New York for a film screening, he would take Sissie along. For the experience to see the world, he would tell his friends. With so much experience, Sissie never found Glenville High School so exciting. In the French club, she sat in the back of the room and thought how she would run things better. She wasn't a homely girl, having many of the same features as Rebecca, the Beauty. Only with Sissie, the mouth went down a little bit, the nose was perhaps a fraction longer, the eyes didn't smile. She insisted on expensive clothes. Some of the prices made her mother look two or three times at

SOUR MARRIAGE, SWEET DREIDEL

the tags. But Maishe decreed nothing should be spared for his Sissie. How else would she find a good catch?

Sissie went to a baseball game! Carnegie Auto Body beat White Motors 5 to 1. Babe hit two home runs and waved to Sissie in the stands each time. The other girls at the game turned around and looked. Who was she?

Behind the scenes, the machinery began to work. Tillie Klein Matchmaker, of Tillie's Dress Shop, got on the phone to friends of both parents. Wheels turned. More phone calls were made. Hints the size of water bombs were dropped.

So the Braverman and Mandlebaum families were joined in marriage. Sissie's father fumed, although he paid the wedding bill. This certainly wasn't his choice. But Sissie was saved the stigma of endless maidenhood, and Mrs. Braverman could look forward to more grandchildren.

Never mind that the couple was not "right for each other." Never mind that this wasn't a marriage made in heaven. It was made by Ohio Bell Telephone. Which of the two got the better of the deal? Who can say? It depends to whom you're related. Personally neither was a prize catch.

So? So, it was a rotten marriage. Out of ten, this would be the runt of the litter. Yet it was a marriage. So it should be saved. But as in so many 'arrangements,' the people who start these things are never around to help when the milk goes sour. They are off starting new castastrophes.

Babe rented for them a small, but expensive, apartment on Lee Road. It was at the end of his route. In order to save money (because Sissie refused to work as it was Not Done in Those Days in Her Circle in Her Image of Her Self) they bought furniture for only part of the living room. A picture, a sofa and a mirror. In the kitchen, they had from his

SOUR MARRIAGE, SWEET DREIDEL

mother a small wooden table with a dropleaf. And in the bedroom, a bed. Wedding gifts were still in boxes. No place to put them.

Marriage had no effect on Babe's daily routine. He was down at the produce market by a quarter to six in the morning because by half past six everything decent was sold. The *drek* would be left for the general public to buy at the city market during the day. By two in the afternoon Babe would be all sold out. He'd come home to the apartment and sleep on the sofa until after five to be rested for baseball. Games started at six thirty. His day was regular, like a clock.

Sissie in the beginning went to all Babe's games. She sat behind first base and tried to believe it was interesting. It wasn't. Baseball bored her as did most sports. But baseball took the cake. The only thing that perked her interest were the girls who hung around the players afterwards. Even Babe. She was jealous, but finally resigned herself to them pestering Babe. After all, what were they? A bunch of blond nitbrains.

She started reading the Saturday Evening Post during games. Then she got headaches in the afternoon, so she wasn't in the mood to go. Then she stopped getting headaches. She just didn't go, making no excuse.

Was it too much to expect, thought Babe to himself, to have a good home-cooked meal once in a while? When he lived with his mother....

And she thought, what kind of life is this? He's never at home and when he is he's asleep.

They kept their feelings to themselves. To admit they had a problem would be to admit they'd made a mistake, nearly impossible for either one of them.

By June 20th at 5:00 a.m. came the first harsh words. Yelling!

"Is it too much for you to get up and make breakfast? I have to get up at five! You think I even get a hello out of you?" he yelled, hoping to wake her up. She turned over and pulled the covers higher. "Are you listening to me?"

SOUR MARRIAGE, SWEET DREIDEL

"Why should I listen? You're acting like a fool."

"A fool! You call me a fool, Ms. High and Mighty! Who do you think puts food on your table?"

"A table! You call that a table?" He had finally opened up a subject she was dying to get into. "My mother wouldn't feed a cat on a table like that! You're too cheap to buy us some decent furniture, like other husbands."

"Which other husbands do you have in mind?"

"Rebecca's husband for instance. Robert Lindsey would be ashamed to let his wife live like this."

"Is he saving for a new truck for his business? Is he? IS HE?" As Babe pulled his shirt on, a sleeve ripped. "Dammit!"

"Another example? Alex Saperstein..." She was getting warmed up.

"Furniture you want? Where would you put it? This apartment is such a mess with papers and magazines and books and boxes piled everywhere. Did it ever occur to you to clean this place up? What in hell do you do all day?"

"What do you think I do all day? ...What *is there* to do all day?" She got up from the bed and started pacing around the room in her nightgown. Now she was like a fighter ready for round two.

"So why don't you get a job? Then we'll have money for furniture. Is that too much to ask? Or are you are you a Queen...a Queen...or something!" He spit out the words, getting incoherent in anger.

"Me? A job? Me! Do you think that's what I got married for? I didn't have to get married to get a job, you know."

He slammed the door and was gone. She was so mad she threw herself on the bed and pounded and pounded at the pillow. What was this thing she'd gotten herself into? It had been so peaceful at home.

"He wanted you to get a job!" bellowed Maishe Mandelbaum. "He actually said THAT?"

SOUR MARRIAGE, SWEET DREIDEL

"Yes, Daddy, yes. I'm telling you. He was like a crazy man." Her eyes were red from rubbing and tears.

"Did you hear that, Flo? Did you hear what our daughter is telling us?" Maishe was incredulous. Flo wasn't, but she knew from long experience the value of silence.

"What does he think I am?" Sissie sobbed, seeking the comfort of her rather's arms.

"Right," said Maishe, "What does he think Sissie is? He expects maybe his wife should be hired out to scrub floors?"

"No. He never said that, Daddy."

"I was only using that for an expression," he assured her.

Nobody knew what else to say. So they all sat down and stayed quiet. After enough of this, Flo finally stood up. "Shall I make us a cup of tea?" she asked timidly.

"Go. Go," commanded Maishe. "What are you waiting for?"

When Flo was gone, Sissie started to explain while holding back her sobs, "He said, Daddy, that if I wanted furniture…a job…because he was saving…a truck for the business…." Her voice broke as she started again to sob out loud.

Maishe stood up. Importantly. "Business is one thing. His home is another. He should make enough money from his business to support his family… or he's no businessman."

Maishe ran a small movie house in the nearby town of Painsville. It was open Thursday through Saturday. This qualified him as a lion of business knowledge.

Flo returned with three cups of tea and served everyone. Nobody thanked her. It was expected.

SOUR MARRIAGE, SWEET DREIDEL

Flo finally volunteered, softly, as if she were afraid she might be heard. "Maybe you're too critical, Sissie. Are you sure you are making him feel good?"

Maishe immediately misunderstood. "What are you talking! Sissie isn't some slut. What is he? What? A cabbage peddler! He should get down on his knees every day to thank God for an angel like Sissie."

Flo persisted, but quietly, "I only meant making a nice dinner once or twice a week. Is that so…"

"Our Sissie isn't kitchen help. If she doesn't want to cook… Does Rebecca cook for Robert Lindsey, I ask you? They have a maid. So why should Sissie be forced to open a restaurant?"

Flo sighed. She should have expected that.

In the months that passed things got no better. Babe and Sissie could hardly talk about anything before an argument started. She spent more and more days visiting her parents.

It started to aaffect Babe's hitting. His average dropped below .250. And in a crucial game against Cleveland Drop Forge he made two errors in the eighth that cost the Rockets the game. They had dropped to third place.

Marty Haines, catcher, team captain and best man at Babe's wedding, asked him to have a beer after the game. Not because Babe loved beer, or Marty either. It was to talk. Marty was trying to figure out what was eating at him. Babe finally unloaded. It was a relief. He'd had no one else to talk to. His mother thought Sissie was a lovely Jewish girl, after all those others. She wouldn't hear a thing against her.

As luck would have it, Marty's sister, Elaine, had trouble with her marriage. Even worse, she had two kids. Marty told Babe they went to a marriage advisor who did wonders for her. Wonders!

"Naw," said Babe, "I couldn't do that."

SOUR MARRIAGE, SWEET DREIDEL

Marty tried to explain, but Babe refused to listen. "I couldn't talk to a total stranger," he insisted.

As the weeks passed, he started getting up later in the morning. Six. Then six-thirty. By the time he arrived at the produce market, the best was gone. The pears were full of brown marks. Celery from Kalamazoo was ragged. He had to cut off the brown leaves at the top before he dared show them to his customers. People on his route started to ask why things looked bruised. He blamed it on the lack of rain this summer.

Babe's batting average dropped below .200. The team sponsor, Mel Hoffmann of Carnegie Auto Body, took him out to breakfast on Saturday morning. Babe couldn't talk to Mr. Hoffmann about personal problems. So the breakfast was a bust.

When Babe was benched, he knew things were serious. He asked Marty for the name of his sister's marriage advisor. On the back of a scorecard Marty wrote *Mother Zaide Schwartz* and the address.

"You want me to see a total stranger?" Sissie was incredulous. "You must think I'm crazy or something."

"Look, you're always jumping up and down about furniture," he said.

"What is this, a bribe?" she asked.

"Just come and we'll see. What harm can it do, Sissie? Things aren't getting any better."

"So why don't you talk to my father? He offered to talk to you." She was pacing around the near-empty living room. This would be so embarrassing, she felt. Going to an *Advisor* meant she had lost control of her life, like she'd been declared "Crazy".

"Your father isn't exactly my idea of someone to talk to. He wants me to offer free dishes on a vegetable truck!"

"Well, it was only an idea to improve your business. You should be thankful he offered to help with all his years of experience."

SOUR MARRIAGE, SWEET DREIDEL

"I'm not running a Saturday matinee! And Cleveland Heights isn't Painsville!"

It took a few more weeks of this kind of argument. Sissie agreed to visit this Mother Zaide Schwartz if Babe promised not to tell her father.

Two days later Sissie had second thoughts. Maybe a separation for a while. She went to see her father, but he wasn't home. So she sat despondently with her mother and waited. Flo and Sissie started an innocent conversation. Before she knew it, the word divorce came out.

"Don't even think about it," Flo said while wiping her eyes. There was a long wait before anything else was said. Sissie watched her mother's face but got no hint of what was behind those brimming eyes. Finally Flo was ready to talk again. "A distant cousin of mine, Ida Rosenthal, a sweet person who also married late. She married a man who was some kind of diamond dealer in New York. He already had two children. Ida was expected to take care of them, naturally. At times he would do some very mean things, but she always took it. Finally one day she didn't take it. She left him and got divorced."

"Suddenly no one would talk to her. Your father, who never liked her husband anyway, forbid me from talking to her. I wanted simply to call her on the telephone. He forbid it!"

Sissie said, "But Momma, that's so unfair."

"Some people think it's a shame if a woman can't live up to her marriage responsibilities."

"But if we don't get along, to have to stay with each other? It's so unfair."

"Tell me about unfair," said Flo as her tears flowed.

The address was on 105th Street, near Parmalee. An old Jewish neighborhood. It turned out to be a small candy store. An orange sign on the window proclaimed HOLLYWOOD CANDY STORE. prop. MOE SCHWARTZ. "Hollywood" was Moe's idea of a catchy name.

SOUR MARRIAGE, SWEET DREIDEL

"This couldn't be the place. A candy store!" said Sissie. Babe showed her the address on the scorecard. "Come on, let's leave," she said, pulling on his arm.

"Wait. Look at that sign." He pointed down to the right-hand corner of the window. A sign there, with letters made of stitched yellow yarn on a black card. Even the smallest letters, stitched. It read:

MOTHER ZAIDE SCHWARTZ
Advice with the Cosmic Dreidel
No Problem Too Small or Too Big for Mother Zaide

Inside the store a small bent-over man came forward. He had a ring of whispy white hair that started in front of his ears and trailed all the way around the back. On top, except for six strays, he was totally bald.

"Something?" Moe asked. "The chocolate creams were delivered fresh today from Hollywood," he said in his finest salesmanese.

"I think we'll just look around," said Sissie. This did not look like a place to get marriage help.

Babe went up to the old man and whispered, "The window sign. Mother Zaide."

Before he could get the rest of the question out, Moe had the answer, "Oh, you mean my *meshuggener* woman! She has her place in the back." Then he shouted as if 'the back' were half a mile away, "Zaide. some people for a *bissel* advice." There was no answer, so he shouted again. "ZAIDE!"

A muffled voice replied. "Moe, I told you never to shout at me. I'm in the bathtub."

"She was advising until late," he explained to Babe.

"Moe? You were calling?" Zaide's smoky voice was closer now.

SOUR MARRIAGE, SWEET DREIDEL

"Is some people for advice, Zaide. A customer!" he yelled through the black floral curtains.

"Wait. I'll put something on. Send them to the studio."

Moe motioned for the two to go through the curtain. "Go up the steps. What God created as a room, she invents into a studio. Wait for her there."

They went timidly through the curtains, and up three stairs. To the right was an alcove hung with oriental-style rugs. The 'studio' was lit with five or six red and yellow bulbs, of the sort fashionable on used car lots or outside picture shows. In the center of the room was a low round table with three chairs. No crystal ball on the table. There was a wooden box, painted in yellow and black Chinese letters. It had a sliding top, making one suspect it once held Velveeta cheese.

"Wait a *bissel* please," Mother Zaide called. "I'm getting decent. Sit. Make yourselves at home." A glass was knocked over. From behind the rug came an expression I won't repeat.

Neither one chose to sit. They looked around the room. Pinned to the hanging rugs in random irregularity were signs.

SUFFER FOR A HAPPY MARRIAGE

SHOW ME AN UNHAPPY COUPLE AND I'LL SHOW YOU A MARRIAGE WITH A FUTURE

IF YOU DON'T HATE YOUR HUSBAND, YOU DON'T UNDERSTAND HIM

A DAY WITHOUT PAIN IS NOT POSSIBLE

MADE IN HEAVEN IS NOT A UNION LABEL

There was more, but that's enough to give you an idea.

In a swoosh the rugs parted and she was here. "Hello, I am Mother Zaide Schwartz. Pleased to be your acquaintance. Darlings, please. Sit!" It was a command and they did. She wore a billowing silver turban

SOUR MARRIAGE, SWEET DREIDEL

around her head, and her ample figure was draped in a flowered print from a South Sea Island. You know how fat ladies love to wear sheets with pictures on them. Her eyes were deep-set and blue, the look of a Siamese cat. A luscious red was pasted on her full mouth. Five short black hairs jutted from the mole on her chin.

"You know me," she said, "but I don't know you." She gave them her throaty laugh.

Babe said, "This is my wife, Sissie, and I'm Babe. Babe Braverman. We heard about you from a friend on my ball team. Marty Haines, our catcher. You helped his sister…" Mother Zaide didn't let him finish.

"My darling boy, I help so many people, keeping track is not possible. You should have called for an appointment. I have many waiting to see me. Am I right? Of course I'm right."

Babe showed her the scorecard. "All we had was this address."

"Of course, my darling boy. I must get cards printed up. Still, call for an appointment. Polite! Am I right? Of course."

"I'm sorry," said Babe, "Next time we'll make an appointment."

Sissie grabbed his arm and pulled him close enough to whisper. "What are you being sorry about? We're customers. We don't have to apologize to her. And what's this with rugs for walls? I mean, Babe, do we really belong here?"

"Excuse me, my sweetheart. I couldn't help overhearing," said Mother Zaide, "If you were so smart, darling, why are you here? If you had all the answers, my sweetheart, you would be spending money at Halle's Department Store instead. You should hold onto your tongue until you know what you are talking about."

Sissie sat back and glared, feeling helpless and humiliated.

"Forgive me, my sweetheart, but Mother Zaide always speaks the truth. My darlings Sissie and Babe. You are here for my help, which I

SOUR MARRIAGE, SWEET DREIDEL

am glad to give. Am I right? Of course I'm right. But first we must be sincere to get help. And how does Mother Zaide know you are sincere? Because you are ready to pay the box." She slid open the top of the box with black and yellow letters. The inside was lined with black felt, making it look bottomless.

A confused Babe said, "Sorry, we don't know how much."

"Of course, forgive me. This is your first visit. Ten dollars. Unless you wish to hear from the Cosmic Dreidel."

"Cosmic Dreidel? What is it?" he asked.

"Forgive me again, darlings." From underneath the table she pulled out a heavily lacquered black cube with intricate filigree designs in gold. The cube had no bottom or top...no opening. As Mother Zaide said "Makhbeyah" she pulled the cube apart. It split along a curving line in the design. From inside she took out a leather bag and a folded piece of black velvet. The velvet she spread slowly and carefully on the table, smoothing out all the wrinkles. Then she loosened the drawstring on the leather bag and let slip out an ivory dreidel.

It rested in the palm of her hand. The moment the dreidel fell from the bag, a light came on from above and flooded the center of the table in brightness. As she showed the dreidel around, it moved from light to darkness to light.

As you know already, a dreidel is a four-sided Jewish top. With it you play an old game, who knows from how many years, of Put and Take. On each side of the top is a Hebrew letter: *Gimmel. Hay. Shin. Nun.* They stand for different actions, like Put Two In The Pot, or Take Two, or Take All. As Babe and Sissie looked closer they could see "age" lines in the ivory, wrinkles. Black Hebrew letters carved into the bone looked as old as the first Torah itself.

"This dreidel knows things," said Mother Zaide, her voice vibrating like a cello. "For centuries it has advised, from Genghis Khan to Rockefeller. The Rothschilds made a fortune from the advice of this very dreidel.

SOUR MARRIAGE, SWEET DREIDEL

"For Genghis Kahn it fell *Gimmel*. Take All. On that advice alone he took Europe. It told Cleopatra *Nun*. No snakes. But would she listen? Willful, nu, see what happened? The same thing it told Napoleon. *Nun*. There's nothing in Russia but trouble. But he knew better. Better than this dreidel? You must be smart to listen to the dreidel. Any dummy can't do it."

"Only yesterday, a big shot businessman. IMPORTANT. His name if I mentioned you would fall out of your chairs. Should he invest in a particular project? Hundreds of thousands of dollars were mentioned. No names. I keep my confidential. Am I right? **Of course** I'm right. This project is so big, even his wife doesn't know about **it. We** asked the dreidel. What did it say? *Hay*. Take Two. What does this mean, the big shot asked Mother Zaide? Invest twice as much I told him. The man turned white. Absolutely white, even with a Miami tan. For him my fee was one hundred dollars. But you are a young couple. For you fourteen only."

She pushed forward the wooden box with the Chinese letters. Babe slowly counted out ten crumpled one dollar bills. At fifteen cents a pound, that was over sixty-six pounds of tomatoes. He looked at Sissie. She nodded. He counted out another four. Until Babe put the money inside, Mother Zaide did not touch the box. She would not taint herself. The box wanted money. She was from another world.

She slid the lid closed and put the box under the table. The Cosmic Dreidel lay in the center of the black velvet, listening.

"So tell me, Darlings, what's on your mind? Talk. Tell Mother Zaide."

I don't have to repeat for you the whole story. They poured out their hurts.

He can't invite his friends, because Sissie hates company. She won't clean.

To which Sissie replied they're not her friends. Babe spends more time with them than with her. He's married to her! To her! Isn't that supposed to mean something?

106

SOUR MARRIAGE, SWEET DREIDEL

To which he replied they've only been married two years and he's known them since Glenville High School. Does she expect him to give up his best friends?

To which she raised her voice. "Your friends are filthy. They don't have sense enough to take their cleats off when they enter a home? All they want is BEER! We never had beer in our house all the time I grew up. I don't think it's even kosher. I didn't get married to be a cook. I don't even have furniture!"

To which he replied that most of the time she goes to her parents, so what does she need with furniture?

They replied and replied and the dreidel listened. When they had nothing more to say, every hurt talked out, both were exhausted and quiet.

Mother Zaide nodded. "Look behind you, my darlings, to where it is written:

SHOW ME AN UNHAPPY COUPLE AND
I'LL SHOW YOU A MARRIAGE WITH A FUTURE

Tell me, is it Fate or is it not Fate? Listen, my Darlings, you remember hearing some words once like 'Forsaking all others'? Do you think they were written by a two-year old donkey? They were put for a reason."

Mother Zaide reached slowly for the dreidel. She looked up to both faces. "Shall we ask the dreidel?" Sissie and Babe looked at each other. They nodded. She reached her stubby fingers out, each with one ring or more, picked up the dreidel by its top, and spun it! "Round and round," she sang in a sing-song voice, "and when it is all tired it will fall down boom."

Shin. Put Two. She turned to Sissie. "Put Two. The dreidel is talking to you, my darling. Put twice. Two times you must make a dinner for Babe's friends."

"No. No, I can't," Sissie cried in terror. Of the three here, she alone knew she'd never cooked a meal in her life. Cooked anything.

SOUR MARRIAGE, SWEET DREIDEL

"The dreidel has spoken, my darling. You must." Then Mother Zaide put the dreidel back in the bag, folded the black velvet and put them away in the cube. "Our time is over, my dears." She rose and left the room through the rugs.

Babe reached over and touched Sissie's arm. "Don't worry. No matter what the dreidel says, I'll help you."

They set a date two weeks away. For Sissie it was like looking forward to a Serious Operation. Having a gallbladder removed. She bought dozens of cookbooks. She called schoolmates.

In the middle of the night she got up and paced. At two a.m. she burned blintzes. When he got up at five, Babe would see messes dumped in the trash. It was impossible to tell what she'd been cooking. If worst came to worst, he thought, he would bring home roast chicken and potato salad from Levy's Delicatessen.

Babe invited Marty Haines and three other ballplayers to drop by after a Saturday game. He warned them. Sissie would be making dinner. If anyone said anything to make her feel bad, they would answer to him.

At the Saturday game, before the fateful dinner, Babe was put into right field when Sam Conroy failed to show up. Babe was so nervous he struck out three times.

Here was the famous menu. See if it wouldn't make you nervous. Raw carrot sticks. Baked stuffed eggplant. She liked the color. Goulash. And apple pie (which she burned. Actually she burned three).

When the men showed up, they took their shoes off at the door and padded around in stocking feet. She made them drink beer from glasses instead of out of the bottle. Mikey White said something funny about the eggplant and Marty threw a fork at him. The goulash had too much paprika. The eggplant—well, you know eggplant. Even a French chef would get laughs from eggplant.

SOUR MARRIAGE, SWEET DREIDEL

But you should have heard the compliments! "Hey, Sissie, this is swell." "More goulash and more water, too."

"My Mom don't make carrot sticks as good as these."

They played their parts well. She invited them back for chicken paprikash, which turned out not a bit better. For the rest of her life, she only made dinner for guests ten more times! The whole rest of her life! She never became a cook.

In a month, they returned to Mother Zaide, because life was far from better… but Sissie hugged Mother Zaide. Sissie told her how the dinner went. Babe thought it was great, but his friends are still drinking water. Babe paid another fourteen dollars for another visit with the Cosmic Dreidel.

What was to be next in their lives? After much flourishing, Mother Zaide spun the dreidel. This time *Hay*. Take Two. What's the meaning? They looked at Mother Zaide. "What's the meaning, my darlings, of Take Two? Sissie will take home any two pieces of furniture she wants. Anything!"

Babe complained that he couldn't afford it, business wasn't that good. Whatever the excuses, the dreidel had spoken, said Mother Zaide. Sissie was pleased. Something was finally going her way.

The very next day she went to Friedlander's Furniture Emporium. They were having a regular Once-In-A-Lifetime Annual Clearance Sale. Only two items. She couldn't decide. Floor lamps? More chairs? Bookcases? She settled on a kitchen-dinette set. With enough chairs. Never again would friends have to stand eating. Sissie chose a special plaid color. At that time very fashionable.

So things were changing. But not much. Many days Babe would come home to an empty apartment. When they went back to Mother Zaide, Babe was adamant.

"If the Mandelbaums want to see Sissie, they should visit our place," he said, "You said forsake all others. So let her start some forsaking.

SOUR MARRIAGE, SWEET DREIDEL

"I don't see you forsaking any baseball," Sissie replied.

"You want to be a boy," said Mother Zaide to Babe, "And you want to be a daughter," she said to Sissie. "This is natural. But not good. What do you think, Darlings, should we ask the dreidel." They agreed.

So what came up? *Nun.* For nothing. What means nothing? "You, Babe, are to say nothing. Sissie will visit in good health her Momma and Papa. Once or twice a week is fine. After all, they were her parents for twenty-nine years before she knew you. But be sensible. It's your problem to work out. Babe will keep his mouth shut. Nothing. *Nun.*"

She looked at Babe. "You are not happy? Good. Suffer for a Happy Marriage."

"You mean this is what marriage is?" he said. "Arguing about visiting parents? Or Sissie getting sick to her stomach worrying about making dinner? Going into hock for furniture? Is this it? We still argue on so many things. She hates my baseball," he said morosely.

"No, I don't hate it," Sissie pleaded.

"Don't kid me. I know you do. And I can't help it. It's what I was happy at, and I'm not happy anymore. My mother wanted me to meet a nice Jewish girl. I did. It looks like that's not enough."

"Darling, for many that's a lot," said Mother Zaide. "Think of me and Mr. Schwartz. What do we have in common? He calls me to taste chocolate creams when they come in. You think he understands from a Cosmic Dreidel? Does he listen to advice? We are two people, locked together in different places. He's in front with Creams and I'm in back with the Cosmic. You hear what I'm saying? We stay somehow together. Am I right? Of course I'm right." she folded her hands, not with self pity, but with resignation. "As the saying goes, Made in Heaven is Not a Union Label."

The two young people looked perplexed. There was such a great weight on things.

SOUR MARRIAGE, SWEET DREIDEL

She patted their hands. "I shouldn't give you my problems," Mother Zaide said with a sad smile. "Tell you what, my darlings, let us ask the dreidel. One more time. This is on me." She carefully lifted the Cosmic top. Her pudgy fingers spun it. "Round and round…" It came to rest.

Gimmel. Take All. So what does this mean, Take All? Mother Zaide appeared speechless with joy. "A Gift. You two have received a rare gift. The dreidel is telling you to take all of each other. Go. Go tonight. Have a glass of wine. Eat a dinner at Shevesy's Hungarian Gardens on East 79th Street. Take All. Tell them Mother Zaide sent you."

She folded up the black cloth with a sweet sigh and put the Dreidel back in the decorated cube. Sissie reached out her hand for Babe. Take All.

What do you think when you hear that, Take All? I see that dimpled blonde little *shiksa* Helen O'Connell singing "…All of me. Why not take all of me…" *Life can be, still, a warm mystery.* Tell me honestly, who do you think of?

What happened? A little less second base and a little more home plate. A little less running to Daddy with her complaints and a little more holding onto Babe. They really did have a good dinner at Shevesy's.

A few days a week Sissie started going with him on his route, on the Willys-Essex truck, meeting his customers. Then she got up even earlier and went to the produce market. Some fruit she wouldn't let him buy. Not good enough. Lettuce she pulled from the bottom of the crate. She picked them over until she got only solid heads with no bruises.

A regular toughy she was in the market. Nothing was good enough for her Babe. The Golden Delicious were too green. Knock off four cents a pound. Celery stalks from Kalamazoo were too dirty. Wash them for me first. She was a pest, but she got her way.

SOUR MARRIAGE, SWEET DREIDEL

Farmers and wholesalers took it as a matter of pride if they could sell to Sissie. Such a tough nut to crack. By and by business picked up. People came to expect that from Babe's Produce truck, only the finest fresh.

She made him buy two stalls at the Cleveland Westside Market. Indoors. Two stalls! He thought she was crazy. They'd go broke. But he put the truck money down on the stalls.

BABE & SISSIE'S FANCY PRODUCE
EVERYTHING FRESHER THAN YOU

I don't have to tell you how it went with them. You can fill in the rest yourself. The dinette, plus a new sofa and chairs and bookcases they paid for without borrowing a cent. They didn't even notice how easy, they were so busy. Sissie kept Babe hustling. He didn't have time for baseball.

To make him feel better, she talked him into sponsoring his own team, Babe's Blues. In his wildest dreams he never thought he could afford it. But he could and did. Who could dream, his name on the uniforms!

Was that a Cosmic Dreidel or wasn't it/ Listen to me, if you ever hear of a sour marriage, I know someone with a sweet dreidel to give advice. Ask. I'll give you one of Mother Zaide Schwartz's cards.

After Sissie and Babe, she had some printed up.

SONG FROM A DREIDEL

It was by accident. I met Mrs. Rabinowitz while shopping for tomatoes at the Farmer's Market on Bank Street. A sunny June day, the kind you wish for. To tell you the truth, it was a total surprise. I hardly recognized her. She looked awful.

I had known the Rabinowitzes, Ernestine and Herschel, for seven…eight years—who remembers exactly? We weren't friends, but I knew them enough to say hello and ask, "How's life treating you?" Of course, since he ran away, I wouldn't dream of asking such a question. A total idiot I'm not.

The last time I saw Ernestine Rabinowtiz was four years ago. Charlotte's house. A fundraiser. The Rabinowitzes were big givers, especially if he could throw his weight around. Excuse me for saying this, but Herschel Rabinowitz when he was wealthy, loved always being right in any conversation. Money can buy you that. When you don't have money, your opinions have to be logical.

SONG FROM A DREIDEL

But back to the story. The last time I saw her, she was gorgeous. Still had her figure at forty, even with three daughters. Still had a knockout smile. Still had the money to buy soft and wavy red hair once a week.

I'll have to admit, privately, that I would have loved to have her on my arm and take her anyplace. But she was married to a big shot, a big shot in the furniture business. Next to Herschel I was, of course, a nobody. I know it, so it doesn't matter if you say it, too.

Here she was standing only one booth away from me, a washed-out, gray-faced, excuse me…an old woman. She must have aged forty years, not four. She avoided my gaze, embarrassed I thought. But I'm not the kind to cut people off when they're down on their luck. A place I've been many times myself. As I came closer, I could see large tears filling her eyes. Her body was without a life force, as if she'd just taken a shock that sucked away her insides.

"Ernestine, what a nice surprise to meet you here," I said. What else would you expect me to say? "You're death warmed over?"

I knew she couldn't remember my name, so I helped her. I asked if I could buy her a cup of coffee. There was a refreshment stand at the edge of the Farmer's Market. She nodded.

While walking there, we passed a strange booth with a gnarled woman sitting in the back, smoking a black cigarette. She looked like someone not from this country. As if you lifted a gargoyle from a village church in Hungary and set her in Kalamazoo at the Market.

A jagged rock lying there on embroidered linen. Her face was as strange as the items she had for sale. Amber and black stone necklaces. Golden apples made of glass. Small bundles of ribbon ends, secured with rubber bands. And incense. Twenty sticks burning in a circle.

The old woman's eyes were hooded like a sleepy goat's. Large hairs grew from a wart on her left cheek. On her upper lip was a mustache thick enough to need shaving. She stirred and looked at me deeply.

SONG FROM A DREIDEL

The goat was awake now. Was she looking at me or at Ernestine next to me?

Ernestine let go of my right arm and shifted to my left, to put distance between herself and the old woman. When the woman saw this, she crooked her finger in front of her nose and shook it. Then she took the black cigarette and flicked the long ash at the end in Ernestine's direction.

A warm June day, so I cannot explain the chill we suddenly felt in the air.

I know Ernestine felt it. She clutched at my arm, as if trying to draw warmth from me. What was going on? Did these two somehow know each other?

We found a small umbrella table at the coffee stand. The shade was nice. But she was shivering. I tried to lend her my sweater. She refused. Not looking at me, staring down, she cupped and uncupped her hands. Delicate hands? Not anymore. Rough flaky skin. Thin red scratch marks on the backs. The hands of someone who scrubbed for a living. Not the hands of Ernestine Rabinowitz? This didn't seem possible.

What am I saying? I should know enough about the world to understand there are no limits to what is possible. The worst can be followed by the still worsee. Take my word for it.

Ernestine told me that in the last hour she'd been drawn by some force to that old woman's booth. She had left it only moments before I picked her out of the crowd. What the woman had told her caused Ernestine's tears.

The old woman knew of Ernestine's bad luck. Or pretended she knew. You understand how fortune tellers work.

Here's what Ernestine remembers the old woman saying. "Many things in our past, they frighten. We try to forget. It does no good to hide. They grow in the dark. Does that make sense, my dear? If it does, give me a dollar, so I'll know you're honest."

115

SONG FROM A DREIDEL

Ernestine said she was too poor to waste the few dollars she had on such foolishness.

"Foolishness!" The old woman had cackled and waved a crooked finger at Ernestine. Just as she waved when we walked past later. "I know you. Your crow has flown away. Am I right? Give me a dollar to prove that I'm right."

It was uncanny, thought Ernestine. How could this old woman, whom she'd never met before, know about her?'

"Your fortune has changed. Shall I tell you why?" said the old woman.

Of course she listened. Could you resist if someone asked you?

"An evil sits on the shoulder of someone in your home. You have children? Ah, daughters. Give me a dollar."

Reluctantly, she handed the woman a dollar. That left only two for birthday presents. But what else could she do?

"One of them is controlled by an evil fortune. Until that child leaves you, you will go down and down until you are in the pit of misery. Nothing you do will change that."

"I can't believe…," said Ernestine.

"Believe! A curse on one of yours."

"… a curse on a … child?"

"A child is at fault. A child!" The old woman hissed, then added, probably to save her skin from the police, "But what does an old woman like me know?"

Ernestine felt caught in a web. She had to ask, "How will I know which …?" Imagine! To be ensnared enough in the thought to even ask such a question about your own child!

"Watch as they sleep. One covers her eyes. She will try to hide, but it will do no good. Evil fortune will follow wherever she goes."

SONG FROM A DREIDEL

Whew! What a story to hear on a sunny June day. Now you understand why Ernestine looked like she'd been run over by a garbage truck.

She lowered her head and said to me, "One of my children cursed? Who ever heard of such a thing? One of my babies!" Heavy tears poured from her. Her shoulders heaved in jerky sobs. Here, under a public umbrella, Ernestine was pouring out the grief she's been suffering these past four years. I gave her my handkerchief.

Unbelievable. Maybe to help you understand, I should share what little I know of the Rabinowitzes. At least what I saw from the outside. Who knows what goes on inside a family?

Herschel Rabinowitz, I knew in good times and rotten. The rotten happened about four years ago.

He was in furniture stores. Three, five, many stores. What he stocked sold like hotcakes. "Furniture like hotcakes?" you ask. Not logical?

Wait. His did. His slogan was "LOWER THAN WHOLESALE. ROCK BOTTOM AND UNDER." And he meant it.

He took from manufacturers their mistakes. Immediately and for cash. I don't mean defective merchandise and seconds. These he refused to handle.

What he bought were good things in the wrong places. As they say, dust is simply matter out of place. Things like special orders for customers who changed their minds. Scheduling mistakes. Over-runs. Herschel always paid cash. For the manufacturers this was wonderful. They never had to warehouse their boo-boos. The stuff never stayed around to raise an owner's blood pressure.

Thus Herschel could offer true bargains. "Look, Mrs. Klein," he'd say to a customer looking at sectionals for her new daughter-in-law, "to save eight hundred dollars, can't you live with plaid?" Of course, she could. He knew it. And she knew it.

SONG FROM A DREIDEL

As Herschel Rabinowitz became richer several things happened, all of which you could predict. His wife got a cleaning woman to come in three days a week. Each time, Ernestine followed her around to make sure she didn't smoke and that she cleaned "underneath as well!"

Herschel became even more of a know-it-all. Nobody could tell him anything. He went on a worldwide buying tour to pick up Persian rugs from Turkey to Taiwan. Who could tell him that Kalamazoo and Grand Rapids weren't ready for two thousand "almost authentic" Oriental rugs? Herschel was one of those guys who had the money to prove himself right.

Money to spend? After his third daughter, Alexandria, was born, guess what he did for her second birthday? He had two tons of sand flown in from Alexandria, Egypt to spread around the swimming pool. To honor his daughter. What a birthday!

But the rugs didn't sell, despite land-office promotions.

Herschel figured with so many people going back to hardwood floors, Persians would be hot. Bad guess, especially at "authentic" prices.

The more they didn't sell, the more Herschel poured into advertising, full pages. Even in the Chicago papers. That wasn't free, you understand.

Maybe fifty carpets in all were sold. And for a steal.

Money got tight. It was a shame this happened at what should have been a joyous time, the first years of his beautiful daughter Alexandria. But business is no respecter of homelife.

Herschel stopped paying "cash immediately."

Manufacturers who had sold Rabinowitz their mistakes started thinking he was one.

The cleaning woman that Ernestine followed around was told to find other work. Mrs. Rabinowitz now could find out how easy it was to satisfy herself by cleaning underneath.

SONG FROM A DREIDEL

Over the next three years, from bad it went to worse. The phone in Herschel's office rung constantly. Creditors wanted to be paid. For a one time Know-It-All, the thought of bankruptcy was not an option. The humiliation he couldn't take.

One Thursday morning, Herschel did the unexpected. Leaving for his office, he gave his wife and daughters a hug that was unusually long. Then vanished.

Disappeared.

His car was found parked at the Amtrak station. In a fifteen-minute zone.

The police were called. With nothing to go on, they assumed Herschel had gone off on a buying trip. It had slipped his mind to mention it.

What slipped was not his mind. What slipped was Herschel. Out of the picture.

Days went by. Not a call. Not a letter. Ernestine went from fear to despair. Her life crumbled. All she had left was her home and three lovely daughters. Without Herschel, the furniture business withered. In two years, the wealth vanished down the drain.

With no money coming in, she couldn't afford the house. The bank took it. She sold jewelry for money to live on. After all, you can't eat diamonds and pearls.

Ernestine moved her small family into the upstairs half of a house on Reed Street, a medium to poor neighborhood. At least on a bus line.

Please don't think harshly of her. Don't be tempted to say, "Probably she deserved it."

Why probably? Does she "deserve" bad luck and not you? You are better than she is?

SONG FROM A DREIDEL

Although Ernestine lived comfortably while her husband was rich, life wasn't all a bed of roses.

Ernestine had a younger sister, a troubled mind. Ernestine loved her, worried for her and visited her often. The more she told her that life was worth living, the more miserable and withdrawn her sister became. Who understood what was gnawing at her? "What do you know!" she would scream at Ernestine from her hospital bed. "What do you know what's in my head. You with your parties and rich husband and swimming pool people? You think I like being in this agony? What do you know of me!"

Then her sister would lie back on her bed, exhausted. Softly she would say to Ernestine, "What did I say? It's so nice to have you come visit. But I'm tired now."

What a terrible shock when her sister cut her wrists! Suicide…who expects such things? Ernestine was pregnant at the time. The shock was so great, she nearly had a miscarriage. A normally active woman, Ernestine was bedridden for over a month after her sister's death.

Alexandria was her sister's name. That's why in loving memory, Ernestine Rabinowitz named her third daughter Alexandria. That's also why they never called her Alexie or Ally or any shortened nickname. Only the full Alexandria would do.

Little Alexandria was given a present on her first birthday, from her dead aunt. She willed her a favorite toy, an intricately carved rosewood dreidel. It made an angelic sound as it spun. This dreidel was created by a famous wood carver from Cleveland, Reuben Abraham.

It was still in its original box. Obviously it had not been used. Why not?

Ernestine Rabinowitz had come to the Market hoping to find one "nice" thing for a few dollars for her youngest daughter's birthday.

SONG FROM A DREIDEL

Three dollars? Five years ago she would have paid that much for the bow on the gift box, to be thrown away.

Her children missed Hanukkah entirely this year. There was absolutely not even a half dollar to spare. She barely paid the electric to Consumer's Power.

Little Alexandria would at least have a birthday this year. How old now? Seven? eight? Four years since she was abandoned by her father, the big shot.

I felt ashamed. If someone had only asked me, I would gladly have given Ernestine something from time to time. You would have too, if you'd known. Am I right? But we don't know such things about each other, and we don't make an effort to find out.

Ernestine was not one to ask. She'd held herself close when she was rich. And she kept herself close now that she was poor.

How did she make a living, what little living she had? You won't believe this—Ernestine Rabinowitz cleaned houses.

With a crooked, sad smile, she told me. "Funny, I'm cleaning homes of women my husband wouldn't let me associate with. They weren't important enough."

What I'm telling next, you won't believe.

If Paul Harvey were a Jew, he would love to finish this story for you. Many of the things I didn't find out until later. Instead of interrupting to say I heard this part from that person, and found another piece from someone else, driving you crazy, (after all, what do you care from whom I heard it? You only want to know what happened!) I'll put it all in one piece. And I'll try to repeat exactly as I heard, from Molly, the pot maker, from that Mexican family, and from the strange fat Cuban and her son. If anyone else knows something, let them tell it to you.

SONG FROM A DREIDEL

THE RUNAWAY

That night, when her three girls were asleep, Ernestine crept into their bedroom. Her heart pounded. "Pray God I see nothing," she murmured to herself.

But there was little Alexandria asleep, frowning, her right arm covering her eyes.

Ernestine gave out an uncontrolled cry. **Her daugh**ter awoke and looked at her.

"Mommy. What's the matter?" said the little girl, rubbing sleep from her eyes.

Ernestine raised her apron and wept. Alexandria, her dearest child, named for her lost sister. This one cursed?

"I had a bad dream, and I couldn't sleep."

"Tell me what the dream was, Mommy. Then I can take the bad dream and you can go back to sleep." Can you imagine a child with such an imagination?

Pretending it was only a dream, Ernestine related the story of the old woman, and what she had said about someone in the family with Evil sitting on their shoulder.

"I understand. Go back to sleep now, Mommy," said Alexandria. When the house was quiet again, the little girl gathered a few things that were precious to her, including the dreidel, put them in a small carrying bag, and went out into the night.

Listen to what I'm telling you! An eight-year-old, alone in the middle of the night!

Alexandria wandered the streets and, God knows how, wound up on Humphrey Avenue, near the hospital. It was just before dawn.

Humphrey has older houses on deep lots. In the back some still have barns. I'm telling you , barns in the city!

SONG FROM A DREIDEL

From one of those barns came a light. People working late or getting up early. A rusted van was parked by the open barn door. Inside you could hear wisecracking. A woman and a man.

Also the clink of pottery and the scratching sound of newspaper wrapping. The two were loading apple crates into the van.

Alexandria stood just outside the spill of light. Watching. Shivering a bit in the nippy night air. Dawn was beginning to freshen the sky.

The woman, Molly, looked up from her work and noticed Alexandria. "Hey, kid. You lost?" Molly had a yellow bandana around her braided blond hair. She wore faded blue coveralls. She was bony and tough.

Alexandria shook her head.

"Where you from?" Alexandria said nothing. "Cat got your tongue?" No reply. "Come on, stick it out and let me see."

Alexandria moved a peep of her tongue through her lips.

"Ah, at least you still got it!"

Her co-worker called to her," You talking to me, Molly?"

"No, Bobby, I think we got a homeless people out here."

Bobby came to look. "Maybe she's just walking in her sleep. She's still got her nightgown on under that jacket.

"You walking in your sleep?" asked Molly kindly.

Alexandria shook her head.

"You wanna help?"

Alexandria nodded, yes.

"Sorry, you can't honey. These are very precious...." She held up one of the lucid blue bowls. "Hello, Gorgeous. I'm going to send you out into the world, and you're going to bankroll groceries for a year!"

Molly turned back to Alexandria, as if to explain. "This is a year's work here, plus what's still in the kiln. If we don't sell a bunch of these

SONG FROM A DREIDEL

today, we're going to be up the creek, paddling in a bathtub. We've finally rated a booth at the Bronson Art Fair. Big deal! Today is payday!" Alexandria nodded, as if she understood, which she didn't.

"Kid, you really look cold. Don't you want to come inside and get warm?"

Alexandria took a hesitant step forward. Molly went out of the barn and took her hand. She led her gently inside.

"All I got to offer you is my last bagel. But we're going to be so rich when we come back, I'll get you a pizza all your own! How does that sound?"

Alexandria lifted a small smile.

Molly told her she could stay by the still very warm kiln in the back of the barn. She and Bobby would return late this morning for another load of pots. And not to worry. They'd help her find home.

The van left. Alexandria took a few small bites from the hard bagel, then lay down to recapture her sleep. The kiln radiated warmth.

Alexandria woke to screaming, yelling, police and fire sirens. The kiln had broken open. Exploded. Pieces of broken blue pots were strewn everywhere.

Alexandria wandered around in a daze. She clutched her little cloth traveling bag.

The fragments of pots were still very hot. Small fires had started where they landed in newspapers or piles of apple crates.

A policeman came and roughly pulled Alexandria away from the barn.

The next door lady pointed, and yelled, "She did it! She's in the gang that runs around here. Destructive animals. She's one of them. Lock 'em up!"

"What's your name?" the policeman asked Alexandria.

She was too frightened to say anything.

SONG FROM A DREIDEL

"Where you from?" More silence.

"Did you start this mess?" She finally shook her head.

"Was you inside the barn?" She nodded.

"Well, if you didn't start it, you know who did. Come on." He grabbed her by the arm and put her in the back of his squad car.

Molly returned, wildly angry. "What happened! What happened to my work!" She was hysterical. A year's work!

The next door lady yelled to Molly, "There was a gang of ten kids. They caught one. Police got her in their car."

Molly rushed to the squad car. She pounded on the side window, her screaming face close to the glass. "You little bitch. YOU UNGRATEFUL LITTLE BITCH!"

Inside, Alexandria cowered. Could she escape? She tried the door on the other side.

It opened. Alexandria ran, clutching her little bag. She ran through the crowd of milling people, vanishing into the coming evening dark.

It was ten that night before she lost her fear of being chased.

On Washington Boulevard, a Mexican family, the Tortegas, had started a restaurant in their home.

It had closed, but all the inside lights were on. Alexandria stood on the front porch and peered in.

The whole Tortega family, Mama Maria, two boys and three girls, were having their own dinner. Missing was the father, Ubaldo, who worked second shift at Fisher Body.

A family restaurant has two advantages. All in the family have enough to eat and everyone has an important job.

One of the boys, Carlos, glanced at the front window. He saw a little girl with matted long hair. She wore a stained rose nightgown. He shook his head at her. "We're closed!"

SONG FROM A DREIDEL

Alexandria didn't move. The rest of the family turned to look at her. Mama Maria asked, "Any of you know that little girl?" No one did.

"Not from around here," said Juanita, a daughter.

Still, Alexandria didn't move. Finally Mama Maria got up and went to the door. "We're closed. You'll have to go home." Still she didn't move.

"Do you understand," the mother spoke very slowly, "we aren't open."

Alexandria just stood there. "Are you lost?" No reply. "Are you hungry?" Alexandria nodded.

The mother unlocked the door, took Alexandria's hand and led her inside.

"Mama, I thought we're closed!" chimed in the other daughter, Mary.

"She's hungry. There's plenty. Tony, move over and make her a seat."

Tony said, "Then she's got to wash dishes, Ma. It's only fair!"

"Hey kid, did you lose your mother?" asked Carlos.

"Sssh, none of your business," said the mother.

Mary said, "She's a runaway. I bet she's a runaway, Mama. We learned about that in school."

"No," said Juanita. "She's a homeless person, I bet."

Tony asked, "Are you on drugs, kid?"

Juanita cut in, "Don't bug her, Tony. Here, kid, have some enchiladas. I made them."

She ate everything they put in front of her. After dinner, she dried pans for the two boys. Then she scrubbed a pile of smaller plates. She was welcome.

A bed was made for her by the storeroom, in the back of the kitchen. Blankets spread on the floor. One of the girls donated a pillow.

SONG FROM A DREIDEL

When Ubaldo Tortega came home at 2 a.m. and found this white child in his home, he was furious. "We got to find out where that gringo kid lives. This ain't no goddam flop house. Get the police on the phone."

"Ssssh," said his wife. "They'll just take her and throw her in jail. What if she was your daughter?"

Well, with one thing and another, they didn't find out the next day or the next. The Tortega girls started teaching Alexandria Spanish words.

On the third night, everything was quiet. Alexandria was snug in her makeshift bed in the kitchen storeroom. Ubaldo Tortega was home from Fisher Body and warmly in bed with his loving wife, Maria. A peaceful world.

Suddenly there was a commotion in the kitchen. The noise was awful. Ubaldo and Maria jumped out of bed and ran downstairs.

Alexandria, in a corner by the stove, was screaming, open-mouthed, at the top of her lungs.

Jars of beans were smashed and spread over windows, stove, walls, and the floor. A bag of white flour had been torn open and thrown everywhere. Bottles of salsa were spilled on the floor. Worst yet, the brass cash register had been dumped on the floor. Keys had been bent out of shape.

Everyone was awake. The children stared at Alexandria in disbelief. Maria cried out, "Mother of God. What's happening?"

Ubaldo clenched his lips. He shook his huge fist at Alexandria. "This is the way you pay us back? You rotten gringo kid. Get out of my place! Get out!" He babbled on and on, pouring out his anger. "I told you, Mama, you can't trust them. GET OUT!"

Alexandria raced for the back door, clutching her little traveling bag. The last sounds she heard were Maria's wailing and Ubaldo yelling "GET OUT!"

SONG FROM A DREIDEL

Ubaldo Tortega's voice trailed off as she ran further into the night.

What was it, a day later? About three in the morning. North of town, along Westernedge by the greenhouses, a Ford station wagon passes a dirt-splattered little girl walking on the road. The driver, a heavy, dark-skinned West Indian named Serito Comargo, talks to her son.

"What's a little kid doing out this time of night?"

"Who cares, Ma?" said the son, Emilio. "Just drive. I wanna get home. I'm hungry."

"Means nothing to you that a little girl's walking out here alone at three in the morning?"

"Why should it? I didn't put her here."

"God put you here. His second mistake."

"Get off my back, Ma. It's a free country," he said. "Ma, please don't slow down and talk to her like you always do. She's none of our business."

A minute or so later, the Ford wagon drove onto the gravel drive of Comargos' small farm.

Emilio immediately began carrying mops, pails and rags into the barn. These needed to be washed and dried for the next night's work.

His mother went to start dinner.

When Serito came out to find Emilio, she saw the same little girl they'd passed on the road. She was half-hiding behind a bent over maple. The yard light glow caught the edge of the little girl's stringy hair.

Serito went to her. "You lost?" There was no reply.

From inside the barn Emilio bellowed. "Ma, who you talking to? Dinner ready?"

Serito ignored him. She touched Alexandria. "You wanna come inside?" Alexandria looked up at her eyes for a long time.

SONG FROM A DREIDEL

Wait a minute! We've been through all this before. Same questions. Same answers. Each time people try to help. Their world is turned upside down. Alexandria is blamed, screamed at, driven away.

Is this to be the rest of her life? A string of bad luck? String? ... an anchor chain we're talking about!

If you've felt sad enough already, you don't have to go on. Only Alexandria has to go on, her Evil Fate driving her.

Inside the Comargo kitchen, the room was hung with shawls, in blues, in greens, in reds. A small one was draped over the kitchen light. The feeling of a warm cave. The table was set for two. In the center was a circle of smoking incense.

Alexandria rubbed her face. "It burns your eyes?" asked Serito. "That's okay. I'll set them here on the sink. Been burning incense long as I can remember. Calms me down."

Emilio paid no attention to the stray his Mother had brought in. He didn't bother to look at her. Instead he was busy with eggs, hash browns and sausage.

Serito made a small plate for the girl. Emilio reached for the last sausage. His mother cracked his hand with the wooden spoon.

"Hey. No fair! Why does she get the last piece and not me?"

"Because you grabbed with fingers instead of a fork. Twenty years old. Ought to know better in front of company."

"She's company? You got to be kidding! She's just a kid ran away from home. What's so great about that?"

"Did you ever have to run away from home?" Seri.to asked him.

"You a runaway?" asked a now curious Emilio.

Alexandria ate a few bites, but said nothing.

"Where you from?" asked Serito. No answer.

SONG FROM A DREIDEL

"Afraid to tell me?"

"What's your name?" Just a stare.

"You don't have to tell me if you don't want to."

She thought about it, then said, "Alexandria."

"Hello, Alexandria. My name is Serito Comargo. That's my son Emilio, who does all the eating."

"Hello…," from behind a weak smile.

"Alexandria. You know where you live?" She shook her head. "Know where you came from?"

"No, they don't want me back."

"Yeh, I know. I've heard that before. Don't worry. They still love you. Got any money?" Alexandria shook her head.

"She's probably hiding a bundle, Ma. I know she raided the mattress before she skipped."

"That true? You got lots of money?"

Again she shook her head, no.

"You got anything?"

Alexandria reached into her bundle and pulled out the dreidel box. Serito opened it and took the dreidel from its velvet bag.

"What's this?"

"A dreidel," said Alexandria.

"What good is it?" asked the woman.

"I don't know. It's to play a game."

"Strange looking thing. Carved all over. Where'd you find it?"

"It was a present from my Aunt. She died."

"Then you got family? Want me to take you home?"

SONG FROM A DREIDEL

"They don't want me." She took a long look into Serito's eyes. If she told the truth, would they throw her out into the cold?

She took a chance. "I cause trouble."

"Why you do that?"

"Do what?"

"Cause trouble. Why for you do that?"

"I don't do anything. But wherever I go, bad things happen."

"Of course, you're a little hell raiser. You get into mischief?" She gave her a knowing wink.

Alexandria shook her head. "No. No. I try not to do anything wrong. But things break or fall over or get all messed up. It's not my fault. But everyone says it is and they yell at me and want to kill me...."

Too much. She broke into sobs. Think of this. A child of eight, chased out into the night ... not once. Three times. Even by her mother. Would you not cry yourself?

Serito put her heavy arm around the little girl. "You want to stay with me a few days? You like to work with Emilio and me?"

Alexandria shook her head, "Something bad will happen again and you'll hit me and chase me away...."

"Don't worry about that. Ain't no bad things to happen while I'm around. Whoever's causing you trouble will have to go through me, first."

Alexandria didn't believe that. Would you? No. But what choice was there?

The work Serito and her son did was clean offices at the CoMerica building in downtown Kalamazoo, at night. While the world slept.

By now you know what to expect in this story. Some kind of explosion will make the morning television. Right?

SONG FROM A DREIDEL

The next night, as they were cleaning offices belonging to a group of attorneys, it happened.

Alexandria was cleaning and polishing a desk top. Serito said she wanted to see from here to Mars in it.

Emilio was working the vacuum. Serito was unloading wastebaskets into a plastic bag in the large conference room. An all-night radio station from New Orleans was playing when it happened!

A Steelcase three-drawer file cabinet tipped over, spilling files all over the floor. Then another started to fall. Emilio caught it just in time.

He yelled for his mother. "Ma, come quick. She's doing it to us!"

Alexandria flattened herself against the wall. It was happening again. Her mouth opened wide and she started to scream.

"Ma! You see! You see what she's doing!"

Serito came running. She saw folders and papers scattered over the floor. Emilio was struggling against an unseen force, trying to pull another large file cabinet over on top of him.

Alexandria was searching for a way to open the window, to jump away. It was six stories up. "Now you hate me, too!" she screamed, as she saw Serito coming at her.

The child's face was changing. Her eyes had a red fire in them. Her mouth was contorted. She was being possessed.

The big woman grabbed Alexandria and pulled her around. "Stand behind me, honey." Then she let out a bellow big as a gospel choir.

"OH YOU. OH YOU. WHEREVER YOU ARE. BETTER GET OUTA MY WAY!"

The air was electric.

"WHOEVER YOU ARE... WHEREVER YOU ARE... YOU GOTTA GO THROUGH ME TO GET THIS LITTLE GIRL. NOW GET... OR DEAL WITH ME!"

SONG FROM A DREIDEL

The lights flickered out. The building was buried in blackness. Even the street lights were black.

"Don't move. It ain't gone yet!" yelled Serito to Alexandria, "Stay behind me!" Then she sang out, "I GOT YOU, SPIRIT. YOU'RE RUNNING NOW!"

They waited long minutes in the dark. The lights came back on.

Back home Serito sat the little girl down at the kitchen table. "You gotta tell me everything you know. Else I can't help you."

Alexandria related what her mother haad said the night she woke up. And what happened at the barn with Molly's burning pots. And what happened in the kitchen with the Mexican family. She swore she was nowhere near the file cabinet when it tipped over.

"You ain't strong enough to do it if you wanted to. I know that," said Serito.

"You're not going to chase me away tonight, are you?" Alexandria pleaded.

"Sssh. Nobody's chasing anyone. You listen to me and do as I say. I'll stay by you till this whole mess is over."

"What you got is an Evil Spirit watching you. That Spirit won't give you up. Unless we do something. For the rest of your life, you won't have any peace."

Alexandria covered her eyes. She didn't want to see the vision, but she listened.

"Now don't worry. You ain't the first one with an Evil Spirit. I had me one. Near drove me out of my mind, 'til I found out it was living with the birds outside my house. Birds! I made a special effort to feed those birds since. Poppyseed cakes. I set 'em out every morning when I come home. If I don't, they make my life hell."

SONG FROM A DREIDEL

"Ford wouldn't start. Mop handles split. Dirt bag in the vacuum would break open and spread dust all over the offices. You wouldn't believe the bad things that happened to me."

Looking for clues, Serito again asked Alexandria to repeat all the details. She mentioned the gift of the dreidel.

"Yeh, I forgot about that little thing. Let's try it. See if anything happens."

Alexandria took it from the velvet bag.

Emilio grabbed it to spin it, because boys know tops. He was still in a rotten mood. That little girl had caused him all kinds of trouble. He was the one who had to push against the "force", keeping that second file from falling over. Did anyone say "Great!" Not on your life.

His mood changed. As the dreidel spun, it gave off an angelic tone, a sweet voice. As if there were a being inside that came alive when the dreidel turned. Emilio was affected. He stopped pacing.

Each time the dreidel stopped, Emilio spun it again. For the sound it made. Serito noticed that as it fell, it always pointed in the same way. South. Back towards the city. But what in the city was it trying to show them?

Serito went outside to consult her birds. After all, Evil must know Evil.

I ask you, does the word "dybbuk" mean anything to you? Can you believe there's such a thing as a trouble-making Spirit? A mischief maker both in and out of this world, a revenge seeker?

Well, maybe... Yes... Possible ... Yet?

Think about it.

The crows led Serito Comargo to the Jewish section of Mountain Home Cemetery on West Main Hill. It lay on a high bluff. You could see as far as the smokestack of Nazareth College.

SONG FROM A DREIDEL

They arrived just before dawn. "We're going to find something strange here, honey. Don't know what it is," said Serito to Alexandria. "Are you afraid to go in?" The girl nodded.

"That's all right. Take my hand. Emilio, you wait in the Ford."

Dawn light was coming on. A red slash lay across the eastern sky. The two of them stepped carefully, to avoid tripping over small headstones.

There! Behind a tree was a hunched-over figure. A "creature". Not a person.

They walked as quietly as they could, not wanting to alarm it.

When they were nearly behind the tree, the head turned.

A face of sorts stared up at them. Deep black scratches of dried blood raked down its cheeks.

From the black hollow of its mouth came "LEAVE ME!" in a moan so heavy you felt the vibration of sound in your bones. The creature raised its hands. The wrists were caked in black clots. Dark blood, like candle wax, dripped down the length of its arms. It was wrapped in a mud-streaked gray gown, torn and ragged. The poor creature was shorn of even the dignity of the grave.

"LEAVE ME." The sound of agony. Then came the gut-piercing screams and cries: "BITCH! BURN! HATE! HIT! TEAR!"... *Venom... Venom!*

The creature didn't stand. Its raised arms shook, like a vibrating whip. Strands of matted gray hair swayed like tangled weeds in a churning river.

Alexandria could not keep from staring. She felt drawn to the creature and somehow pushed away at the same time. Her heart shuddered. She could hear drumming in her ears.

"Afraid?" asked Serito.

"No. Yes." She was frozen at a cliff edge.

SONG FROM A DREIDEL

"Well, there's your spirit. Tomorrow we come back and visit again."

As they turned to go, it screeched "LEAVE! FIRE! FIRE! ... LEAVE ME!..." The sound echoed against the cemetery hill as they picked their way back to the Ford.

It was nearly dawn.

The next night they returned, an hour or two before dawn. The two of them came with soap, combs, towels and water.

The creature was still where they'd seen it the night before. It watched their approach. "GO! LEAVE ME!"

When Alexandria tried to touch it, it snarled and lashed out with claw-like fingers. She tried again. The creature flung its arms like a trapped animal hoping to escape the snare.

Serito shook her head. How to calm it down? Then she remembered the humming dreidel. She asked Alexandria to take it out. Carefully, she removed the carved dreidel from her pocket and spun it on a nearby flat gravestone.

The creature watched. As the dreidel spun, an angelic voice again drifted out of the spinning toy. The song of the dreidel washed over the creature. That deep darkness in the eyes closed over. The tight agony in the lips relaxed.

Alexandria began to wash the creature's face and arms. From time to time, it pulled away from her. But as Alexandria worked, she talked to the creature... talked as a young girl might to her doll, or a pet horse. Alexandria washed and combed the creature's hair. It was fine and soft, reaching down over the creature's shoulders.

The scratches on the creature's face remained. But on its wrists, all that showed were the clean-edged scars where the knife had cut.

Dawn was coming. The two left. This time the creature didn't cry, "LEAVE ME."

SONG FROM A DREIDEL

The next night they returned with a clean scented gown. Alexandria had woven a flower garland of wild daisies.

Again the creature refused to be touched until they spun the dreidel. Its spinning voice calmed the air.

The torn shroud was cut away and they put on the clean gown. Alexandria combed the creature's fine hair again as she spoke softly about this and that. "I only have one doll left you know. Her name is Marcie. All my other dolls got lost away when we had to move...." On and on Alexandria talked... The creature's deep black eyes slowly closed.

"Is this always my Evil Spirit?" asked the little girl when she stood up to go.

"Oh yes, for a while. But we'll keep coming back, to show we care. It will be a while," said Serito.

They started to leave when Alexandria turned. "I almost forgot." Alexandria went back to place the garland of flowers on the creature's head.

As she knelt down, she heard a voice, as if coming from within the creature. No lips moved. Nor did it stir.

The Voice said, "You are called Alexandria?"

"Yes. I'm named for my aunt, whom my Mother loved."

"A nice name, Alexandria," said the creature. "Be good to it."

So I ask, why would you tie the living to the dead? To name a child after a suicide? Does this make sense? To have given this child such pain!

As they were driving home, Alexandria asked Serito if maybe Emilio, who always seemed to be in a bad mood, maybe he had an evil spirit chasing him.

SONG FROM A DREIDEL

"No. He's just got a mean mother on his back. No spirit. She's all flesh and blood."

How does such a sad story end?

Should I tell you Alexandria goes home to the open arms of her mother and sisters?

Shall I tell you her father returns next Wednesday a rich man?

Shall I tell you Molly, the potter, becomes famous for her Blue Pots?

Shall I tell you that little Alexandria has nothing but good luck the rest of her life?

What would you believe?

To tell you the truth, none of that. And some of that.

Because if the future was so simple, this would be a fairy tale.

Would I waste your time on a fairy tale?

A DREIDEL FOR VICE PRESIDENT? YOU MUST BE KIDDING!

A dreidel for Vice President? You must be kidding! I'm not kidding. It happened. It's still happening. If I hadn't told you, you wouldn't know it yet. How could it happen? Easy. Of course, not any dreidel could become Vice President. Only a special one. But I'm getting ahead.

How did it start? We are in the back of Schwartz's Texaco playing poker, our gang of Cleveland bums. We gamble. Let me explain. It's a hot June day and the air compressor is pounding. Even though we're not lawyers and doctors, we make an honest living. We gamble. Let me explain. We're a regular group of guys.

In the back of Schwartz's Texaco on Cedar in Cleveland Heights, we have a room. Six of us meet for poker once a week to trade our money. Two are married to crabs. The rest unhooked, thank God. The room?

A DREIDEL FOR VICE PRESIDENT? YOU MUST BE KIDDING!

A place we cleared from spare wheels, brake drums and water pumps. A kitchen table, covered with felt. Folding chairs, an old Frigidaire, a hotplate for tea, a shelf to hold mustard and corned beef. Paper plates for the potato salad, plus other stuff I won't bore you with. All in all, a place of iniquity. A gambling den!

Sometimes I win. Sometimes Garson Feldman. A few times Miltie Kay, but not often. Always Shelly Chance wins. He's got some kinda luck. Shelly is smooth. I'll give him that. Unlike most of us, he's never worked a day in his life. But he makes out. His black hair is always smoothed. Nothing out of place. It must be oiled. Shelly leans to blue cashmere sport coats and silk underwear. Don't ask me how I know. I know, that's all. Ladies who are familiar…talk.

But the point? The point is, today Shelly Chance is losing at poker! Three eights, normally good cards, lose to a full house from Miltie Kay (Miltie Kay who NEVER wins). Later Shelly's full house loses to a club straight, which I am amazed to hold. Me, a guy who normally feeds the pot while eating corned beef. ME. I BEAT SHELLY CHANCE. When Shelly loses to me, something's going on more than luck.

"It's six months till Hanukkah," says Shelly, "Let's play a little dreidel." Miltie groans. I groan. Even big Manny Hertzberg groans. Shelly pulls out a carved ivory dreidel from a brown suede bag marked "Caeser's Palace." The bag is for dice. Shelly…just because he's Shelly…carries his dreidel in a dice bag. Does this make sense? To play with a dreidel in June? Of course not.

"Shelly," I say, "Play poker. If my luck holds,. I'll get even with you by Hanukkah."

"I'm tired of poker," he says. "It bores me. A game of dreidel is more interesting. The odds are always four to one." Not necessarily. Just because a dreidel has four sides? With Shelly Chance, I think, the odds are with whatever's in his pocket. In spite of what I say, Shelly spins his dreidel on the green table. The rest of us are worried. Something's up.

A DREIDEL FOR VICE PRESIDENT? YOU MUST BE KIDDING!

Shelly knows what's up. The rest of us know we're in the dark. Garson Feldman picks up his money and starts putting the twenties in the back and the ones up front. When anyone starts putting their money in a logical order, they're getting ready to split.

Garson says, "I got an appointment to get my Lincoln waxed and shampooed." An appointment! He gets his car waxed every two weeks. He won't park his Lincoln in tight spaces. He'll drive around a half-an-hour to find a double space. He treats his Lincoln better than married guys treat their wives. Nu? He's still single.

Miltie Kay is also piling his dough neatly. Today he's finally winning. Finally! He wants back into a poker game which no longer exists. Miltie pulls his herringbone tweed cap from Halle's Men's Store down over his eyes and fumes. Shelly meanwhile is calm as usual. He leans back in the folding chair, spinning his ivory dreidel.

Miltie is thinking, "Is my luck transferable? Should I risk playing dreidel with Shelly and lose back everything I won?" You can read his weasel face like it was a menu at Sand's Delicatessen. Miltie isn't so rich he can take losing back sixty-three dollars with a smile. Miltie works sometimes for H & R Block. The busy season is over. He lives now off unemployment.

"Doesn't anyone want a simple five card stud?" Miltie begs. He begs! After all, how often does he have luck?

Garson wants to leave while he's ahead for the first time in a year. With his big winnings, he needs a reason to duck out before the rest of us have a chance to get even. So he changes the subject. "I can't understand you guys," says Garson, "Our country is in the middle of an election for president, all you can think about is poker. I'm disgusted with you morons. Don't any of you schmucks read the paper? Listen to the radio? Watch television?"

"I watch the Indians play," says big Manny Hertzberg.

A DREIDEL FOR VICE PRESIDENT? YOU MUST BE KIDDING!

Everybody looks at him and groans.

"Manny, our country is two trillion dollars up the wazoo. The Japs are going to own your *putz* next year," says Garson building up a head of steam, "and all you can think about is a lousy baseball team! I can't believe it."

"How come you didn't give a s—t when you were raking in the pots?" asks Shelly. Garson's face turns red.

"Calm down, Gars," says Miltie, "The election is six months away. Besides, what can six Jewish guys do from the back of a Texaco station? We're not politicians."

"Right. It's too complicated," says big Manny. "At least with baseball, at the end of nine innings, I know who won."

I chime in, something I rarely do. I'm not a talker. "In politics my Uncle Willie says one side gets to be president. The other side gets to be Senators. Nothing gets done cause they can't agree, and then they split up all the money between them."

Nobody pays attention to what I said. Except for Shelly Chance. He keeps spinning the dreidel. Then he says, "Politicians don't agree because they don't know their ass from second base. They fumble around just like we do. They pretend they're smart, but they're not. They don't have answers. I bet this dreidel here comes up with more right answers than all the politicans…and it's just a dreidel."

We all look at Shelly and kinda shruggs. Is he making a joke? Miltie laughs his small weak laugh. "Oh, sure. You want me to believe your dreidel knows more than the President?"

"This dreidel knows more than Bush, who wants to be president," says Shelly. What a strange look he has on his face. I don't know what to believe.

"I know you're kidding," Miltie couldn't tell. "I know you're kidding…aren't you kidding, Shelly?"

A DREIDEL FOR VICE PRESIDENT? YOU MUST BE KIDDING!

Shelly looks him straight in the eye. "...knows more than Bush, than Dole, than Jesse, than Dukakis, than...you name the guy. I'll stack Danny Dreidel against any of them."

"I'm sure," says Miltie cleaning off his glasses, "More than a president, Shelly? Are you for real?"

Shelly spins the dreidel again. When it drops, the letter *Nun* comes up.

Very slowly, even quietly, Shelly says, "How much you wanna bet?"

"Bet? Bet what?"

"This dreidel will become so famous for being right, they'll want Danny for Vice President."

"Awe come on, Shelly. Be serious. We're talking serious here," says Garson.

Shelly comes back with, "I'm talking serious. Serious money. I'll bet you five thousand."

"At what odds?" Miltie asks.

"Twenty to one don't seem out of line. Especially since you think I'm nuts. Twenty to one either the donkeys or the elephants will want my friend, Danny Dreidel here, in their corner."

"Awe come on, Shelly. Be serious...." Miltie felt shakier. Was he walking into a trap?

"Five thousand, Miltie. Put up or shut up." He looks around, "and anyone else can buy in...same odds. Danny Dreidel. Twenty to one. Five thousand."

What we hear is "Let me think about it" or "...I'll let you know tomorrow" or "...You're really serious?"

Shelly nods. Yes, he's damn serious.

Miltie turns to the rest of us, "I can't believe this guy! I can't believe him. Is he serious?"

A DREIDEL FOR VICE PRESIDENT? YOU MUST BE KIDDING!

I kinda believed him. Kinda! Before I knew it, I was saying, "I'm in with Shelly and the dreidel for a thousand."

Everybody looks at me. I'm supposed to have some sense, because I went all the way in temple through bar mitzvah to confirmation. What was I saying? Where was I going to get a thousand dollars to bet on a cockamamie dreidel?

Stop. Let me explain something. By now some of you guys out there are asking "What's a dreidel?" Fair question. A dreidel is a four-sided Jewish top, played with at Hanukkah time by children. A game of put and take. I said children? Also by adults who think luck is a quicker way to get rich than working.

On each side of the top is a different Hebrew letter. *Gimmel, Shin, Hay* and *Nun*. At the beginning of each round, everyone feeds the pot. A nickel, a quarter…three quarters. With Shelly, it would be five dollars. Each person takes a spin. When the dreidel falls, one Hebrew letter is, of course, up, which tells you what you do. What do the letters mean?

Gimmel—Spinner take the whole pot.

Shin—Spinner ante up again.

Hay—Spinner take half the pot.

Nun—Do nothing. Spinner doesn't put or take.

Where was I going to get a thousand dollars! I went home to see my mother. Of course, Uncle Willie was there, reading Spinoza by the kitchen table. Who understands Spinoza? One human being in the whole world. My Uncle Willie thinks he does. But he can't explain it to me.

I went home, but I don't live at home. My mother still keeps my old room for the once-in-awhile I stay. Actually I have a small apartment off Lee Road that I share with Garson Feldman. I come to see my mother when I want dill pickles or I have a problem. I explained to her what I'd done. As I talked, I felt like an idiot…trusting a dreidel with my hard-earned cash!

A DREIDEL FOR VICE PRESIDENT? YOU MUST BE KIDDING!

"So boychick, you're worried about betting on a dreidel?" my Uncle Willie says, looking up from Spinoza.

"I'm not betting on a dreidel, Uncle Willie. I'm betting a dreidel can be a politician. Yeah, when I say it out loud it sure sounds like a dumb idea."

"You could do worse. A dreidel is wiser than you think," he says knowingly.

"That's crazy," I say.

"Listen to your Uncle Willie, Bubbee," says my Mother, drying dishes from dinner. "Your Uncle Willie is a scholar!"

"Mom, this isn't books. This is real life…running a big country. Responsibility. We don't know about such things."

"Look, Bubbee," my Mother says, waving a spoon at me, "I make three meals a day, plus noshing. The house is clean and the heat is always turned up. At the end of the week, everything is paid for. Is Nancy Schmancy Reagan doing better in real life?"

"Mom, I could lose a thousand dollars!"

"Don't worry, Bubbee. If your Uncle agrees, God will provide," she says in her trusting way.

"Nephew, trust in the cosmic concept of a dreidel. I will explain it to you once. Pay attention. The dreidel has four sides. Four. It could have had three sides or six. But FOUR! Let me explain. A square has four sides. Four. An important number. For the Passover seder, doesn't a child ask his father four questions? You think that's an accident?"

"Four! Why not forty-four? Surely if the Bible were written by the SAT people, they'd come up with a hundred and forty-four questions about Exodus. Questions even a Spinoza couldn't answer."

"But a child asks his father FOUR. The sides of a dreidel? Again four. Am I repeating myself? Four Hebrew letters…they mean *A Great*

A DREIDEL FOR VICE PRESIDENT? YOU MUST BE KIDDING!

Miracle There. Do you get my meaning? A dreidel can make miracles. Follow me? Life is four questions."

"Uncle, what are you talking? Life…Life! What four questions?" I was a little irritated by now, at the mystic mishmash he was handing me. Instead of one word answers, he always gives me paragraphs.

Let me explain my Uncle Willie. He's a thin little man, who I don't always see eye-to-eye with. A book reader from way back. He worked maybe two months in his life in a pants factory which he hated. He was luckily hit by a streetcar. The motorman was luckily drunk. Luckily plenty of witnesses. The company settled. Uncle Willie got a lifetime pension which enabled him to read books without interruption. He is my mother's brother. He is a Scholar. Thus he is blessed and can do no wrong in her eyes.

For her to make a pot of cholent or an apple pie for her brother she considers a blessing from God. After a huge meal my Uncle Willie might give her a nod. That's all the thanks she needs. My mother is blind, but she's my mother.

"The wisdom of FOUR is galactic," my Uncle Willie went on. "In Life there are only four important questions. Everyone either asks them or is expected to answer them. Depending. And what are they, you ask?"

I didn't ask.

"Question one: 'Is it a boy or a girl?'

"Two: 'So wiseguy, what did you learn in school today? Nothing? How do you expect to make a living with nothing?'

"Question Three: 'What, you're still not married?'

"And Four? Unbelievable! 'You didn't hear your Uncle Joe died?'

"The whole story. A lifetime in four questions."

"See," said my beaming Mother, "How much your Uncle Willie knows!"

A DREIDEL FOR VICE PRESIDENT? YOU MUST BE KIDDING!

Useless! I couldn't stand it! I had to get out of there. So I took a quart of pickles and left.

Two days later we met behind Schwartz's Texaco to find out which one of us still had kishkas. Who were just talkers and who put up dough. A lot of hemming and hawing and the odds went from twenty to one to twelve. Still pretty good. Some other guys heard about the bet and wanted in for what looked like easy money. It didn't take us long to have fifteen grand committed. We'd have a good haul, if we won.

Where did I get my grand? Uncle Willie. He bet his next two months pension on the dreidel. So, it was Shelly and me against common sense. After everyone leaves I ask Shelly to show me please how a dreidel is going to make a political decision. "I don't question your judgment, Shelly. I'd just like to know since it's my money, too."

"Give me a question," he says.

What did I know to ask? Well read I'm not. What I know about the presidential race is from TV. This was the middle of June. I'd heard Dukakis was going to have a rough time with Jackson. Jackson was second or third in votes. But he was acting like already the Gold Medal Winner. Was he looking for some deal?

"Shelly, from the dreidel I want to know what Jackson wants to settle. Is that a good question?" I ask.

"A great question. It's what politics is all about. Letting push come to shove. I'll spin Danny here."

He spins the dreidel on the green table. The dreidel finally falls. What side comes up? *Hay.* Take half.

"There's your answer. Jessie will settle for half. Half the money. Half the committees. Half the TV time."

"Awe, that's just a fluke. Spin it again, "I say."

A DREIDEL FOR VICE PRESIDENT?

Shelly spins the dreidel five times. Each time it comes up *Hay*. Is this a fixed dreidel?

I change the question. "Ask the dreidel how much Bush should raise taxes to pay off the national debt?

Shelly spins. This time it comes up *Nun*. Nothing. Don't raise them at all. "Spin it again," I say. Each time now it comes up *Nun*. Do you know what the odds are for that! Impossible. The dreidel is saying to me, "How stupid can you be? How many times do I have to tell you?"

The skin on the back of my neck gets gooseflesh. Shelly isn't kidding!

"Shelly, this is one smart dreidel!" I slap him on the shoulder.

"Of course, I only bet on sure things."

"So what do we do next?"

"Well, to be Vice President, we've got to get ourselves a president."

Let me tell you. I work pushing fruits and vegetables for Tom Rinni Wholesale. My territory is the stands at the West Side Market on West 25th Street. I make friends, encourage grocers to carry only Rinni's produce. It's not hard work. half a day maybe. They like me …a Jew working for a dago… makes people laugh. I keep the stands in line.

How? Well, years ago it was a rougher business. Delivery trucks would be pushed over. Lye would be thrown on cabbages. We don't do that anymore. Tom is a good businessman. No rough stuff. If they don't agree, we get the Health Department to close them down. Of course, I knew my way a little around the Wards and City Hall.

I wanted to give Dukakis first chance at the dreidel. A couple of my best stand owners are Greeks. Shelly says Dukakis wouldn't know what to do with a dreidel. No imagination. "Please, just let me try," I say.

Through a contact of a contact I got somebody in Metzenbaum's office to contact a contact with Dukakis. You know how it goes. Phone calls this. Phone calls that. Finally a guy who sounds English, you

A DREIDEL FOR VICE PRESIDENT?

know, a big shot calls me back. "I'm supposed to call you. What's all this about?" he demands.

How could I explain on the phone? He'd hang up by the fifth word. I told him he's got to come see us. We have an inside track on who should be Vice President. Guaranteed to win the presidency. If he don't come, we'll go right to Jackson.

I say, "Someday you'll thank me." He never did.

Shelly and I fly to meet this guy in Pittsburgh. At the United lounge we reserve a room to talk. Who meets us? A young punk called Odie McNally. Was he important! In the first three minutes he makes sure I heard "Harvard Business School" at least seven times. Shelly does the talking. "We have a dreidel that is amazing. It can give right political answers eight out of ten times. It could be a special advisor to Dukakis. If he listens to the dreidel, he will win. No doubt about it."

As he talks, even I am convinced all over again. We had something there! But Odie NcNally? When Shelly says "dreidel" I can see Odie's eyes glaze over. Can you imagine what was going through that Harvard Business School mind? He thought maybe we knew important Greeks so he didn't just walk right out.

"I'll speak with the governor. Generally he's not supportive of things that aren't scientifically verifiable. I don't think you'll find drindels in that category.

"Dreidels," I correct him, even though it means nothing. He is a lost cause.

"I got it right here. Give it a try?" asks Shelly.

"Sorry, I've got another flight to catch."

"So you're from Harvard?" I ask Odie, as he's putting on his topcoat.

"Business School. MBA. '84," he arches his forehead to help me know it's important.

A DREIDEL FOR VICE PRESIDENT? YOU MUST BE KIDDING!

"You ever read Spinoza?" I ask innocently.

"Vaguely remember him. Undergraduate philosophy," he mumbles in a way that says he doesn't remember.

"Spinoza was big on dreidels," I tell him. "My Uncle Willie reads Spinoza for lunch." I thought that might bring him down to earth. It didn't.

"Jerk," said Shelly after McNally left. We both knew the governor would never hear about us.

"What is this?" I ask. "Are we selling snake oil?"

"I did you and your Greeks a favor," says Shelly. "Let's not waste anymore time."

When we get back to Cleveland, Shelly calls in a few bets. We get a phone call from State Republican Chairwoman, Helen Bradley. She talks on and on, but is no help. Hell, I know more people than she does. Ever talk with someone like that? Blah blah about this famous person and that. All the while you know damn well they've never met any up close. One time, just to see their reaction, I'd like to say "Yeah, Howard Baker was over for dinner the other night. He drank too much and threw up." As I said, she was no help.

Tom Rinni gets me to a Teamster VP in Washington, as a favor. I didn't try to explain to Tom what was going on. Tom can think lettuce. Not dreidels.

Phil Coppersmith calls, one of Bush's advance men. He agrees to meet us at Clankey's, a little bar across from the market. He was coming to Cleveland anyway. The minute he walks into Clankey's I know what he is. Something about him. He was big, over six feet six and weighed two fifty plus. Big like Manny Hertzberg, muscles sprinkled with soft fat. When he started to talk I was sure of it. He was a bagman! They'd sent a bagman to talk with us. A collector from Unions and Corporations. Money for the party. Protection. Surprised? Sure I was.

A DREIDEL FOR VICE PRESIDENT? YOU MUST BE KIDDING!

Surprised to find out national politics is just like running the West Side Market, only bigger.

When Shelly says we want to pick the Vice President, Coppersmith laughs. "From hick Ohio?"

I stand up and put out my hand. 'Phil, it's nice to meet you. But you're a bagman. We need to talk to somebody on the high inside." Well, he gets huffy and puffy and he is going to blow us all in. Instead he goes out to collect from the National City Bank. Why was it so hard to find somebody who understood what we had, a politician's gold mine?

We are getting to nowhere fast. Then I remember I know a guy who works on the Cleveland Plain Dealer, Sollie Weintraub. We went to Glenville High School together. Sollie gives me a name, Joe Wyemaster. Joe would be hard to get. He's on the inside track, a real advisor to Bush. And I can use Sollie's name. Joe Wyemaster? I had to find him quickly. How? Because I was in a hurry, I did what was logical. I put a call into the White House. When the lady answered, I asked for Joe Wyemaster. As if I knew the guy. "One moment please."

While I'm waiting on the line I'm thinking this is unbelievable. A little Jewish nobody from East Cleveland is calling the White House as if I have real business. Like the dreidel says, a Great Miracle is Happening Here.

Of course, he isn't there. "Where can I reach him?"

"He didn't leave his itinerary. Would you like to leave your number?" What number should I leave? Home? Do I want my mother to answer from the White House? My apartment? If Garson answers we'd lose him.

I give her Tom Rinni's office. There's always someone on duty to take produce orders. "Tell Mr. Wyemaster that Sollie Weintraub of the Cleveland Plain Dealer told me to call him about a machine to control spin."

A DREIDEL FOR VICE PRESIDENT? YOU MUST BE KIDDING!

You wouldn't believe it. Two days later at four o'clock, a call from Joe Wyemaster. "What's this all about?" he asks, of course. I repeat what Shelly and I decided to say.

"It's hard to explain, Mr. Wyemaster. You know spin control? This is even better. It makes its own spin. Sollie said you'd understand. If I can't see you in three days, I've got a promise to take it to the Dukakis people. I assure you, it's worth a trip."

He bites. He'll meet us at Stouffers on the Square tomorrow. It always works. If you plant the idea they could lose being first…it's irresistible. They always bite.

We take a room. When he comes, we have Wyemaster sit down on the edge of the bed to make him feel uncomfortable. Shelly does the talking, "Look, Mr. Wyemaster…can I call you Joe? What I'm going to show you, you're first going to say it's a trick and you'll want to throw us out of the room."

"Don't do that. Throw us out later, if you want. But first see what a SMART DREIDEL can do for you. You talk about "spin" in your business. This is real spin…."

I'm glad Shelly did the explaining. He's better than I. Besides, he and Joe hit it off. They were the same kinda guys. Bright upstairs. Gambling in their hearts. And they were willing to listen to cockamaymee ideas. After all, in life who knows? What was cockamaymee ten years ago today everyone wants one. Who'd think sensible people would buy guns to shoot paint at each other? Or sunglasses with little lights that blink? Cockamaymee? But it sells!

"…Now, Joe, I want you to think of something in your line of work, that you don't know how it's going to go over. What position should your candidate, Vice President Bush, take?"

"Like what?" asked Joe.

A DREIDEL FOR VICE PRESIDENT? YOU MUST BE KIDDING!

"Like the national debt. Everyone's concerned, right?" Joe nodded. "What is Bush going to do about it? Raise taxes a little to get it paid off?"

"We've thought about it. But we don't like the idea," he said.

"Yet it might make sense to the voters, right?" He nodded again. "So let's see what Danny Dreidel says you should do."

Spin! The dreidel drops. *Nun* comes up.

"*Nun*," says Shelly in a hoarse voice, "*Nun*."

"What does that mean?" asked Joe.

"It means nothing. No tax increase."

Joe was interested, but not convinced. "Let me try it. I'll ask a different question. How about Jesse Jackson? Will he get all the black vote?" He spun the dreidel. *Shin* comes up. "What does this mean?"

Shelly smiled. "*Shin*. That means you've got to ante up. You've got to find a black Republican. You've got to get into their game."

"Let me try the other side. If I'm Dukakis, how do I get Jesse to play with instead of against us?" He spins the dreidel. What comes up? *Hay.*

"Which means?" ...he turns to Shelly.

"*Half.* You have to give him half the pot," says Shelly with a smile. Joe Wyemaster slaps his knee.

"I like the way this dreidel thinks," he laughs out loud. "Wait a minute. This *contra* thing is giving us fits. The press wants to know was Bush in the loop or out of the loop. He can't be in two places at the same time. But how important is that to voters?"

"Try it," says Shelly.

Wyemaster spins the dreidel. When it falls, the letter *Nun* comes up. *Nun.*

A DREIDEL FOR VICE PRESIDENT? YOU MUST BE KIDDING!

Joe nods. "*Nun.* I know it already. It's saying 'Do Nothing.' Not enough voters care." Just to be sure, he spins it again. Even I hold my breath. Will it change its mind?

The dreidel stops. *Nun.* 'Do nothing,' just as before.

"I like it. What do you call it? A dreidel?"

"Danny Dreidel…for Vice President," says Shelly as if it were the most natural thing in the world.

Joe looks first at Shelly, then at me. A cloud comes over his grin. "Now you're not even talking sensible. Up to now you guys have been sensible. But now you're talking nuts. A top for Vice President?

"Too Jewish?" I ask. "Maybe we could call it Danny Quaidel. That's not a Jewish name."

"Joe. First. Do you like the Dreidel?" asks Shelly.

"Of course, it's a great gimmick. Might even be useful."

"Well, we've got two hundred thousand invested here that Danny Dreidel runs for Vice President. If you don't want Danny, we'll take him next door."

"Shelly, the money is no problem. I can get that for you in two hours. I can sell Danny Dreidel as a consultant. But Vice President? …they'd laugh me out of town."

"What if we got someone to front for Danny?" said Shelly. "Someone you could trust to keep his mouth shut. Then whatever strategy the dreidel suggested, he'd get the credit. We just need a candidate who fills space."

"What a minute," Wyemaster interrupts. He looks at me. "What was that name you came up with?"

"I didn't know? What name?"

"The one that wasn't Jewish."

A DREIDEL FOR VICE PRESIDENT? YOU MUST BE KIDDING!

"That was a joke. Danny Quaidel."

"Right," says Joe. "There's a young senator that I think Bush would go for. He's a friend of Teeter's. And I owe Teeter a favor. This senator will look good to George. Nothing great upstairs. We make him believe he has great political instincts. Maybe…just maybe."

I meet this Senator Quayle. He's like a plaster door. But he looks good. And he's willing to go along with the plan. For a chance to be Vice President he'd have learned *Yiddish*. In two days, two hundred thousand is delivered in 20's and 10's. That much money weighs like a ton of bricks. If Tom Rinni could see me now, he'd give up produce and get bar mitzvahed.

Everything goes through Joe Wyemaster. He askz questions. Shelly spins. After the convention, the senator is kept out of sight. Joe makes sure he is always flying between "here" and Louisville or between "here" and San Diego. If a reporter gets too interested in meeting Quayle, Joe takes him to a fancy restaurant and gives him some tinsel. He'll throw in a few quotes about how important Quayle is in strategy sessions.

"The senator seems to know instinctively the pulse of the American people."

Things go beautifully for a month. Our dreidel is calling the right shots. And the senator is getting a reputation as a political hot shot. People say, "So, he ain't such a dummy after all."

But Quayle is getting tired of playing second fiddle to a top. He is feeling his oats, like an actor who forgets he didn't write the script. So he corners Wyemaster and me one night in the backroom of Republican headquarters in Wheeling, West Virginia.

"I'm tired of always doing what a dreidel says. I'm as smart as a dreidel, aren't I? Listen, I've been working on this speech for a couple of weeks. Wanna hear it?

A DREIDEL FOR VICE PRESIDENT? YOU MUST BE KIDDING!

"See, it starts out by me saying 'We're all part of a family. Some of us are from big families. Some from small families. Some of us have no families at all. Even so, families are important. Whether you have one or not. Which ever that may be. And that's what I think about America!"

"Well, what do you think?" he asks proudly.

"About America?" Joe Wyemaster looks at him with the eye of a tired high school coach. "What did you say?"

"You heard. I said we all have our family and aunts and uncles…things of that sort. To be America."

Joe shook his head, "That's nothing but a bunch of cotton balls, Danny. You didn't say a damned thing."

"Yes, well a twelve-year-old kid liked it. He asked me the other day at a shopping center, wasn't I too young to be Vice President."

"A twelve-year-old liberal? What did you answer?"

"I said, America wants a younger person, who is even part of a family. Which is an important American value that everyone can identify with. And that's me."

"So what does that mean?" Joe wasn't very smooth hiding his frustration.

"It means you, you know. American. Younger. Me?"

"No it don't. It don't mean s—t. Now stay out of sight and don't go matching wits with any twelve-year-olds."

"But…."

"Nothing. Danny. But nothing." Joe's voice started to rise "Trust the dreidel. It'll make you a hero. Just don't think for yourself."

Danny was about to interrupt him.

"Please, Danny!"

A DREIDEL FOR VICE PRESIDENT? YOU MUST BE KIDDING!

Maneuverers and advisors and big thinkers are calling from all over the country. Ask Danny this. Ask Danny that. Nine times out of ten, it came out good advice. Which in politics is more than a hundred percent.

To win our bet, Wyemaster let us bring in Miltie, Garson and Manny to listen to the phones one night. The look on their faces could have stopped a truck. I wished I had a camera.

It was a big time experience. But looking back I'm not exactly proud of what we made the dreidel do, just to win a bet. We met a lot of people I wouldn't want my mother to find in her kitchen. It was one of those times that you say, when it's all over, "So? ...what good did it do?" My share was a lot of money. True. But I wonder did we pick the right guy?

Funny thing, about four days after the election we get a call from Joe Wyemaster. He say he's been playing around with the dreidel just for fun, and it's starting to come up with different answers. Like the one about taxes. *Nun* still comes up..but now once in a while a *shin*, too. What does this mean, he wants to know.

Shin. Means ante up. Danny Dreidel is saying put something into the pot. Don't always TAKE. Give something back. Even a dreidel can become a mensch.

There's a lot I can't say because it's classified. TOP SECRET. Red letters across the page. That kind of stuff. At least you know Danny Dreidel is still spinning behind the scenes. Tough questions don't faze him.

Shin: ante up.

Hay: take half.

Gimmel: take all.

Or *Nun*: do nothing.

Do nothing. I'm afraid to say, that comes up an awful lot.

Martin Gal was born in Cleveland and did go to Glenville High School.

There the similarity between life and fiction ends. He, with his wife Jean, is a professional story teller, using stories in this volume as part of their repertoire. Another joint project was to have five children and seven grandchildren, scattered from Boston to San Francisco.

These stories are among fourteen that were created annually as a Hanukkah gift to friends, all somehow weaving a dreidel into the plot. Better than just sending a card.

Kalamazoo is home now, the true Gals from Kalamazoo. Martin is a part-time realtor, a rabbinic aide at the Reform Congregation, and is addicted to paddleball. He and his wife Jean lead English and Country dance groups throughout Southwest Michigan.

OTHER BOOKS FROM ALEF DESIGN GROUP

Being a Blessing: 54 Ways You Can Help People Living with AIDS
Rabbi Harris R. Goldstein. AIDS will not go away. This amazingly simple book by Rabbi Harris R. Goldstein leads us through both the understanding and the actions needed to live up to the best of our intentions. Included are things as varied as "AIDS 101" and understanding what it means to be created in God's image; from how to visit a person living with AIDS to learning the "people with AIDS Bill of Rights." ....Paper Trade. 160 pages. $13.95

Soul Stories and Steps
Trudy Ettelson, Ph.D. Jews have a long tradition of weaving their own stories between the lines of the Biblical text. This embroidery of the Bible is called Midrash. In this collection of original stories, Trudy Ettelson weaves her own understanding of the Jewish tradition, not only around the Biblical text, but around the 12 Steps as well. Here is a spiritual book steeped in Jewish tradition, leading one along a path toward recovery.
....Paper Trade. 128 pages. $6.95

Eight Nights, Eight Lights
Rabbi Kerry M. Olitzky. In this joyous and reflective work, Rabbi Kerry M. Olitzky provides families with a way of letting their Hanukkah celebrations affirm not only their Jewish identity, but the very Jewish values they wish to transmit to their children. For each night, Rabbi Olitzky creates a process of celebration which includes the lighting of candles; the reading of a piece of Hanukkah history; the discussion of a Hanukkah value and a sacred source for inspiration and insight. ....Paper Trade. 64 pages. $8.95

40 Things You Can Do to Save the Jewish People: Some really practical ideas for parents who want to raise "good enough" Jewish kids to insure that the Jewish people will last at least another generation
Joel Lurie Grishaver. An insightful book on Jewish parenting, 40 Things is based on the failures and successes of the author's friends' attempts to be perfect Jewish parents. It is a practical book about improving the odds which asks: "How much can we get away with and still raise fully Jewish children who will in turn raise other Jewish children?"
....Paper Trade. 256 pages. $16.95

The Kosher Pig: And Other Curiosities of Modern Jewish Life
Rabbi Richard Israel. Illustrations by Shan Wells. This unique book of essays explore the tension between being a traditional Jew and being a modern American. Included are essays on: *yarmulkes* and baldness; kosher airline food; hospitality; and synagogue life. ....Hardcover. 160 pages. $18.95

ORDER FORM

I would like to order the following books:
____ Being a Blessing: 54 Ways You Can Help People Living with AIDS................................$13.95
____ The Kosher Pig and Other Curiosities of Modern Jewish Life..$18.95
____ 40 Things You Can Do to Save the Jewish People $16.95
____ Soul Stories & Steps $6.95
____ Eight Nights, Eight Lights..$8.95

Name _____
Phone _____
Fax _____
Address _____
City _____
State/Zip _____

Shipping $4.50, four books or more $5.50.
California residents, please add 8.25% sales tax.

I have enclosed a check for $_____

Please charge my order to: ❑ VISA ❑ MASTERCARD ❑ DISCOVER ❑ AMEX

Cardholder's Name _____
Card Number _____ Expiration Date _____

ALEF DESIGN GROUP
4423 FRUITLAND AVENUE
LOS ANGELES, CA 90058
(800) 845-0662
FAX: (213) 585-0327